CW00376038

OSLO&BERGEN

Part of the Langenscheidt Publishing Group

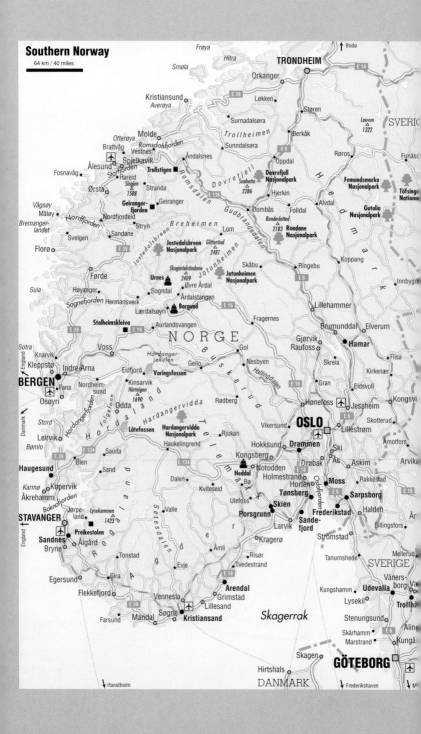

Southern Norway

64 km / 40 miles

Welcome!

This guidebook combines the interests and enthusiasms of two of the world's best-known information providers: Insight Guides, who have set the standard for visual travel guides since 1970, and Discovery Channel, the world's premier source of non-fiction television programming. Its aim is to bring you the best of Oslo and Bergen in a series of tailor-made itineraries devised by Doreen Taylor-Wilkie.

Although Norway's cities are often overlooked by visitors, who are more attracted by the superb surrounding landscapes, they are well worth visiting. Until recently Oslo was a rather quiet, provincial capital; however, the discovery of North Sea oil changed it forever and, although its population is only half a million, Oslo buzzes with life. Bergen's long tradition as a fishing harbour and trading station has made its citizens outgoing and cosmopolitan. In the 13th century it was capital of a united Norway, and is still called the 'Fjord Capital', with its steep cobbled slopes and seven hills that hem it in to the sea.

In this guide, the first three itineraries for each city are full-day tours linking the cities' highlights. Following these are other options, intended for visitors with more time; for those who want to explore further afield there are two excursions, including 'Norway in a Nutshell', a whirlwind tour of some of the country's most beautiful spots.

 The late **Doreen Taylor-Wilkie** was a native of Scotland, which, as she always said, has a striking kinship with Norway (though the fjords are deeper and the mountains higher in the latter). Her aim in this guidebook was to share her great enthusiasm for two of Norway's most notable cities.

C O N T E N T S

History & Culture

From the days of Vikings to the emergence of a modern state boasting one of the highest standards of living in the world, an introduction to the forces and personalities that have shaped Norway's history............**10–17**

Oslo Itineraries

Eight itineraries guiding you through all aspects and sights of Norway's scenic capital city.

1 Oslo Today is a morning stroll taking in the principal landmarks of central Oslo, followed by an afternoon Fjord cruise **21**

2 Historic Oslo explores the sights of Christiania, the old heart of the city, as well as The Museum for Contemporary Art, ending the day at a concert at the Konserthus **27**

3 Bygdøy Day takes the ferry over to Bygdøy island to see the various museums, returning to the city for dinner at a choice of fine restaurants **31**

4 In the Marka is a day in the open air of the Nordmarka, the forested hilly area to the north of the city with fantastic views **36**

5 Vigeland and the Bymuseum visits the charming neighbourhood of Frogner with its lively ambience and street cafés, taking in a couple of local museums en route **38**

6 The Munch Museum and Botanic Garden makes an afternoon's excursion to see the work of Norway's greatest painter, plus a visit to the beautiful botanic gardens **39**

7 Art and Museums is a morning itinerary to guide you around Oslo's main museums in the heart of the city..**41**

8 Afternoon Shopping provides a tour of the city's premier shopping destinations, from modern malls to charming old streets thronged with specialist shops **42**

Bergen Itineraries

Six routes to help you get the most out of Bergen, combining panoramic views, picturesque streets and historic sights.

9 Bergen's Past focuses on the oldest part of the city, from the Torget harbour square to the attractive narrow streets around Bryggen..............................**47**

Pages 2/3:
Oslo on
National
Day

10 Bergen Overview combines a look at the heart of the city with a scenic train ride and a harbour cruise **51**

11 Galleries and Museums explores Bergen's central museums and the National Theatre followed by a walk along the Nordnes peninsula to the Buekorps Museum and the Aquarium **55**

12 Grieg's Troldhaugen is a morning or afternoon spent at the composer's home at Troldhaugen, with a visit to a stave church on the way back into town **59**

13 Gamle Bergen visits the village of Elsesro where a reconstruction shows what Bergen must have looked like in the 18th and 19th centuries **61**

14 Fløyen travels by funicular railway to the mountain behind Bergen, with spectacular views across the city and the coast...**62**

Excursions

Two excursions exploring further afield, the first a whirlwind tour of Norway's most beautiful scenery.

15 Norway in a Nutshell is a guide to Norway's steepest, highest and most beautiful scenery........................**64**

16 Lysøen is a cultural and musical day on this charming island in Lysefjorden, 30km to the south of Bergen **66**

Shopping, Eating Out and Nightlife

Up-to-the-minute tips on where to shop, eat and stay out late **68–78**

Calendar of Special Events

A complete list of Norway's main festivals and holidays **80–1**

Practical Information

All the background information you are likely to need for your stay, including a list of hand-picked hotels..**82–90**

Maps

Southern Norway 2   *The Marka*...........................36
Oslo...............................18/19   *Bergen*...........................44/45

Index and Credits 92–5

Pages 8/9:
The waterfront,
Bergen

HISTORY

Norway is both one of the youngest states and the oldest nations in Europe, an unknown, shadowy region until the Vikings burst out of Scandinavia just over 1,100 years ago. The sightings of their sleek ships inspired first wonder then terror along the coasts of Northern Europe. Thousands of years before, early hunters had begun to push north in the wake of the retreating icecap. As the climate warmed, they settled and became farmers, their legacy being magnificent rock carvings such as those in the northernmost county of Finnmark, and a fascinating 4,000-year-old carving of a skier in Nordland, a replica of which hangs in the Ski Museum in Oslo.

Bronze Age carvings

The Vikings later became Europe's greatest explorers, adventurers and traders, venturing east as far as the Black Sea, west to Britain and France, around Scotland, to Ireland, and then north to Iceland and Greenland, reaching North America in AD1000. Later they became colonisers; anyone with a name that ends in 'son', 'sen', or 'sun' is very likely to have Scandinavian ancestry.

The Vikings' skill as ship-builders was remarkable. Their longships were so fast and manoeuvrable that they could outrun any enemy, yet shallow enough to be run up on to a beach before the luckless inhabitants knew what had hit them. A number of these longships survive in the Viking Ship Museum in Oslo.

Some kings and chiefs became Christian converts. Håkon den Gode was the first, a reformer and law-maker who fought hard against the heathen gods; but his imported missionaries and their sober saints had little success against the attractions of the old Norse gods. Olav Trygvasson, who followed, fared no better and

Culture

it was left to King Olav Haraldson to complete Norway's conversion. Olav lost his life at the battle of Stiklestad near Trondheim, and was recognised later as a saint, when his body was found intact with hair and nails still growing. Norway's first great cathedral, Nidaros, in Trondheim, was erected over his grave and became a place of Christian pilgrimage.

Christianity brought its industrious monk-chroniclers to keep records, but the best accounts of the Vikings come from saga writers such as the Icelander Snorre Sturluson. Undeterred by a century-long gap since the last Viking exploits, he wrote down the old tales that had passed from royal *skald* (storyteller) to *skald,* tales that laud the heroic deeds and warlike qualities of the chiefs and make splendid, if one-sided, reading.

The Vikings were a highly successful and ordered society, and, by the end of the Viking era, Norway was a great power, with colonies in Greenland, Iceland, Scotland and elsewhere. Around AD900, Harald Hårfagre successfully vanquished a mob of chieftains to become the first king of the Norwegians. Haraldshaugen,

The gold of the Vikings

with its giant obelisk, is Norway's national monument. According to Sturluson, the monument marks the spot where Harald Hårfagre was buried, a mile north of Haugesund on the sea route between Bergen and Stavanger.

Cultural Beginnings

Temporary peace came to Norway in the 13th century, a period of great prosperity. Under Håkon Håkonsson and his son Magnus Lagabøter (the Law-mender) the beginnings of a distinctive culture emerged in which art and religion flourished, a good example being the Baldishol Tapestry in the Museum of Applied Arts in Oslo, and the country's trade was vigorous. Then came the Black Death, which entered Norway in 1347 through Bergen, the great trading city that had brought in the wealth. At least half – some historians say two-thirds – of the population died, leaving corpses unburied and graves untended. The country starved, farms lay derelict, and fishing boats began to crumble along the shoreline.

Also instrumental in subduing Norwegian commerce was the stranglehold of the Hanseatic League, the German merchants who monopolised the trade of the north European cities in which they flourished. Though Oslo also had its Hansa merchants, Bergen was their 'capital'. The League ran Norway's trade from the Hanseatic wharfhouses in Bergen for their own profit and Norway, after a time of internal strife, sank into a union with Denmark.

The Baldishol Tapestry

Danish control followed the 'reign' of the remarkable Queen Margrethe, a Danish princess who married King Håkon VI when she was only 10. But Norway and its monarch were impoverished and Margrethe's husband and her father, Valdemar of Denmark, often at loggerheads. When Valdemar died, Margrethe secured the future joint throne of Denmark and Norway for her son, Olav, and became monarch in all but name. The Danes invaded Sweden and, after fierce fighting and even fiercer treachery, the 1397 Kalmar Union united the three Scandinavian countries for the first and only time. The Union lasted for more than 100 years, before Sweden broke away. Norway stayed in the Union, first as a near equal partner, a status that soon deteriorated into what Norwegians call 'The Four Hundred Year Sleep', when their country became little more than a province of Denmark.

The Big Sleep

During those somnolent centuries, Norway was converted to the Lutheran faith, grafted on by Denmark almost before Norwegians had had time to assimilate Roman Catholicism and break the last links with the fierce Norse gods. Danish links with Norway were finally severed after the Napoleonic Wars, when Frederik VI of Denmark, who had been on the losing side, was forced to hand over Norway to the Swedes as the latter's reward for supporting the allies. Norway's reaction to being handed over like a parcel from one state to another was unenthusiastic. On 17 May 1814, in a gathering at Eidsvoll, some 70km (43½ miles) north of Oslo, a hastily convened assembly hammered out a constitution that drew on the political experience of Britain, France and America. It nominated the Danish Governor of Norway, Prince Christian Frederik, as king. Oscar Wergeland's painting, *The National Assembly at Eidsvoll, 1814*, in the Storting (Parliament) in Oslo pictures the solemn scene.

In retaliation, Karl Johan of Sweden gathered 70,000 battle-hardened troops and marched into Norway. The lightly armed Norwegians had no chance. An August armistice led to a new treaty, which put Norway under control of the Swedish crown but left the Eidsvoll Constitution intact, giving Norway its own Parliament. Nothing could stop the Norwegians turning 17 May

Line-up in front of the Storting

into an annual Constitution Day, which nowadays is celebrated in a whirl of Norwegian flags. In 1829, the king sent troops to break up the celebrations but, though the soldiers won that particular skirmish, the king lost the battle. By 1864, the Norwegians were singing their own national anthem, with words written by the patriot-writer Bjørnstjerne Bjørnson.

The Great Exodus

Trade suffered when the common market with Denmark disappeared but the second half of the 19th century was also a time of expansion, freer trade and the start of Norway's astonishing railway network over some of the most difficult terrain in Europe. It also saw a great exodus from Norway when thousands left the country in search of work and prosperity.

In 1825, the first emigrant boat to the New World, the 16.5m (54ft) sloop *Restauration*, left Stavanger with 52 people on board. The first 'sloopers' went largely for religious reasons but others were in search of fertile land. Many settled in Illinois and, although most outward traces of Norway have now disappeared, their influence is woven into American culture and brings Norwegian-Americans in their hundreds back to the 'old country' every summer.

Alongside emigration, re-awakened nationalism grew swiftly, fed by artists and intellectuals. Among them were the dramatist Henrik Ibsen and writers such as Alexander Kielland and Bjørnstjerne Bjørnson. The great violinist Ole Bull and composer Edvard Grieg did much to revive patriotic feelings through their rediscovery of West Norway's traditional music, as did the Polar explorer Fridtjof Nansen, who became Norwegian Ambassador in London. His ship *Fram* forms the centrepiece of a special museum in Oslo.

Near Bergen, the homes of Grieg and Bull remain much as they left them, and Kielland's family home in Stavanger is also open to the public. Towards the end of the 19th century, King Oskar II and the Storting disagreed. The ensuing crisis led to a referendum. The Norwegians voted overwhelmingly in favour of independence and Oskar II had little choice but abdication and retreat to Sweden.

14

Statue of Ibsen

Independence at Last

The prime minister who led Norway into independence was Christian Michelsen, a Bergen lawyer and shipowner. In 1905, Norway became an independent monarchy, with the Danish Prince Carl as elected king. Carl adopted the title King Haakon VII and for the first time in 500 years, Norway was truly its own country. The early years were exciting and prosperous, and then came World War I. Norway was determined to stay neutral and, at first, her sea trade brought great financial gains. Later, with most of her merchant fleet under charter to Britain, neutral Norway lost half its tonnage and some 2,000 merchant seamen. Their memorial stone stands alongside the fjord near the Sjøfarts (Maritime) Museum in Oslo.

Between the wars Norway was hit by the Great Depression and the Labour Party grew in popularity and strength, but its quest for equality and social welfare had to wait until after World War II. Norway's declaration of neutrality did nothing to save it. On 9 April 1940, German forces attacked and for two months the Norwegians

Oslo metal workers circa 1890

fought back. There were successes such as the sinking of the German heavy cruiser *Blücher* but the odds made the outcome inevitable. The Storting refused to appoint the German's choice of governor, Vidkun Quisling, the Norwegian Nazi, whose name became a synonym for traitor. The king escaped to Britain, where the government in exile continued to function in London.

Thousands of Norwegians also escaped to fight on. There were heroic episodes, the most famous being the Norwegian commando raid on the heavy water plant at Rjukan, which ensured that Hitler lost the race for the atom bomb. The film *Heroes of Telemark* was based on this episode. Resistance brought reprisals. Akershus Fortress in Oslo became a prison and has a memorial stone to Norwegian Resistance fighters shot by the occupying Germans. It now houses the Resistance Museum. Around 40,000 were sent to prison or concentration camps such as the notorious Grini on the outskirts of Oslo.

At work on an oil platform

King Haakon returned to his country five years to the day after he left. His tireless efforts while in exile had cemented the relationship between the King and his adopted country, a bond that continued with the popular King Olav V, and his son Harald. Norwegians are extremely patriotic and on Constitution Day the capital's fervent celebrations are concentrated on the long street that leads to the Royal Palace.

After the war, Norway moved swiftly towards a political system based on the Scandinavian model of social democracy which combines capitalism with comprehensive social welfare. The country now has one of the highest standards of living in the world, with prices to match. The discovery of oil in the late 1960s took the economy almost over the top. Norway was awash with oil riches, and towns like Stavanger became international as British, French and Americans moved in. Soon the whole of the west coast, shared in the new prosperity.

Norway joined in the burst of materialism that permeated the 1980s everywhere and, today, is still grappling with a period of over-dependence on oil. Fierce argument over entry to the European Community roused Norway's powerful fishing and farming interests to fury and this led to a referendum in the early 1970s. The vote went against membership. In a repeat referendum in 1994, Norwegians again chose to turn down membership of the European Community.

Historical Highlights

Prehistory Norway settled by primitive hunting communities, about whom little is known.

AD

793 Vikings attack Lindisfarne, off the east coast of England. Viking raiders reached most of Europe in the next 200 years.

9th century Harald Hårfagre creates political organisation and becomes first king of Norway. Christianity gradually accepted.

1028–35 Period of Danish rule, followed by civil war.

1066 Harald Hårdråda mounts an expedition to claim the English throne but is killed in battle.

13th century Period of peace and prosperity under Håkon Håkonsson and his son Magnus Lagabøter (the Law-mender). Trade flourishes through membership of the Hanseatic league.

1262 Iceland and Greenland both accept Norwegian sovereignty.

1347 The Black Death sweeps through Norway, killing up to two-thirds of the population.

1397 The Union of Kalmar brings Norway, Sweden and Denmark together under one monarch. Danish Lutheranism prevalent in Norway.

1523 The Union is dissolved, but Norway is still ruled by Danish governors. Norway enters what it calls the Four Hundred Year Sleep, when timber and fish become the mainstays of the economy.

1814 A Norwegian assembly at Eidsvoll creates a national constitution and the Storting (parliament). Constitution Day (17 May) becomes the most important day in the Norwegian calendar. In retaliation, Karl Johan of Sweden invades Norway, encountering little resistance. Norway is ceded to Sweden, but its own parliament is allowed to remain intact.

1825 The first ship leaves for the New World, sparking great emigration. Nationalism starts taking root.

1828 Henrik Ibsen is born.

1884 Storting given real power.

1898 Universal male suffrage is granted.

1905 Union with Sweden is dissolved. Danish Prince Carl becomes King Haakon VII. A liberal government introduces women's suffrage and social reform and maintains neutrality in World War I.

1920 Norway becomes a member of the League of Nations.

1940 Germany invades Norway in the early years of World War II. The King escapes to Britain. Puppet government imposed under Vidkun Quisling, whose name becomes a synonym for traitor.

1945 Both the monarch and government-in-exile return after the end of the war. Norway is one of the founding signatories of the United Nations (UN), and goes on to join the North Atlantic Treaty Organisation (NATO).

1957 King Haakon dies. King Olva V assumes the throne.

1960s The discovery of oil in the North Sea boosts the economy.

1972 Norway votes against joining the European Community in a referendum (and again in 1994).

1980s Oil wealth brings previously undreamed-of prosperity.

1991 King Olav V dies. King Harald V takes over the throne.

2000 Oslo celebrates its thousand years and Bergen is nominated a European City of Culture.

2001 Crown Prince Haakon Magnus marries Mette-Marit Tjessem Høiby in August.

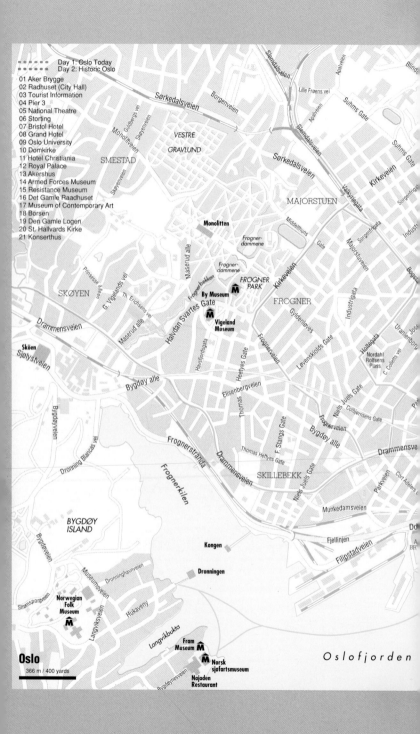

••••••• Day 1: Oslo Today
••••••• Day 2: Historic Oslo
01 Aker Brygge
02 Radhuset (City Hall)
03 Tourist Information
04 Pier 3
05 National Theatre
06 Storting
07 Bristol Hotel
08 Grand Hotel
09 Oslo University
10 Domkirke
11 Hotel Christiania
12 Royal Palace
13 Akershus
14 Armed Forces Museum
15 Resistance Museum
16 Det Gamle Raadhuset
17 Museum of Contemporary Art
18 Børsen
19 Den Gamle Logen
20 St. Hallvards Kirke
21 Konserthus

Oslo

366 m / 400 yards

OSLO IT

O slo is one of the most manageable capitals in the world, with a compact centre easy to wander through and many green parks and forested hills to explore. The Danish King Christian IV can take the credit for laying the modern city's foundations in 1624 but 7,000 years earlier its enviable position at the head of the Oslofjord had attracted first hunters then farmers and traders.

Oslo wharf

Early Oslo, built by Harald Hårdråda in the 11th century, lay to the east of the modern city. Håkon V Magnusson, who made Oslo his capital 200 years later, built a fortress on the site of the Akershus Slot. In 1624, the wood-built town burned down and was rebuilt by Christian IV under the walls of Akershus Slot. Called Christiania after its founder, its lattice of wide streets forms the basis of modern Oslo. Freedom from Denmark brought a flourish of fine 19th-century buildings. The city spread westwards towards the parliament building, the Storting, the Royal Palace and beyond. since the 1980s Oslo has changed its style from small, sleepy capital to bustling city.

Oslo is a 'green' city, which means you pay a toll to bring in a car. The centre is easy to get around on foot and the integrated transport systems – bus, local train, tram, ferry – whisk you in less than half an hour into the hills, forests and fjords. For serious sight-seeing invest in an *Oslokartet* (Oslo Card), valid for one to three days, at a cost of around 180–410NKR. For transport queries, try the *Rutebok for Oslo* available from Trafikanten, the information centre at Jernbanetorget *(see Practical Information p.84)*.

1. Oslo Today

A morning walk from the central thoroughfare Karl Johans Gate, where Edvard Munch and Henrik Ibsen used to stroll, to the Stortorvet marketplace and the Domkirke (Cathedral). From the National Theatre and the Storting (parliament) to lunch at Aker Brygge or a café on Karl Johans Gate. In the afternoon, a Fjord Cruise. Dinner in Wollans, followed by late-night music at Smuget.

Few Oslonians would deny that the best approach to Oslo is by boat, up the fjord to the busy harbour. Failing that, make an early sight-seeing tour by water. Most tour boats and some ferries leave from **Pipervika**, the harbour in the heart of the city. Opposite Pipervika is **Oslo Rådhus** (open Monday–Saturday, 9am–4pm, Sunday 12–4pm; tel: 22-86-16-00; admission fee; guided tours Monday–Friday 10am, 12pm, 2pm), the City Hall, a massive russet-coloured building with two square 1930s-style towers. This is where the Nobel Peace Prize is presented and it is well known for its beautiful frescoes and other fine contributions by prominent Norwegian artists.

Colour in Oslo's city centre

To reach Rådhus from **Karl Johans Gate** (the central thorough-fare) turn south into **Rosenkrantz Gate** and head for the sea to **Rådhusgata**, then turn right. The **Tourist Information Office** (tel: 22-83-00-50 or for 6.56NKR per minute per, call 82-06-01-00) is in the yellow building to the right (Vestbane Plassen 1).

Walk back up to Karl Johans Gate once more and stroll along this broad pedestrian street, the main artery of modern Oslo running from Jernbanetorget train station with Oslo S (Oslo Central) at the eastern end, right up to the Royal Palace (Slottet) at the other. For much of its length, it is free of vehicles and crowds browse along pavements crowded with gaudy little stalls.

The area has some of Oslo's best restaurants, and cafés that move outside in summer. Pick the one which feels the most inviting to you. There are also time-honoured hotels such as the Grand with an ex-

View from the Karl Johans Gate

cellent view of the comings and goings of the Storting (parliament) when it is in session, the Hotel Bristol just around the corner in Christian IV's Gate and the Hotel Continental, a popular hostelry for visiting VIPs, located across the **Studenterlunden** park on **Stortinget**, which runs parallel to Karl Johans Gate.

From the pedestrian end nearest to Jernbanetorget, you come almost immediately to **Stortorvet**, the market place, with its bright stalls of flowers. On one side is the **Domkirke** (the cathedral) consecrated in 1697, after a fire destroyed its predecessor. The ruins of an even earlier cathedral, **St Hallvard's**, named after Oslo's patron saint, lie to the east of the city at **Gamle Oslo**, where the first city stood. Before going in to the Domkirke take a look at the stone relief to the right of the main entrance. It is believed to have come from St Hallvard's, and dates from around AD1100. The 1718 tower clock is Norway's oldest. The bronze doors of the main entrance, which illustrate the Beatitudes, are by Dagfinn Werenski-old, and were added in 1938.

Inside, the cathedral is decorated in greys, blues, greens and gilt against dazzling white, and very Scandinavian. Though the interior owes its appearance mainly to a restoration completed in 1950, this clear brilliance is typified by the organ front which now surrounds a modern organ. The stained glass windows are the work of Emanuel Vigeland. However, it is the ceilings that compel the eye. Painted 1936–50 by Hugo Louis Mohr, they show Biblical scenes

such as the Flood and the Destruction of Sodom and Gomorrah, and episodes in the life of Christ.

Behind the Cathedral is **Domkirkeparken**, a peaceful, sheltered spot where you can sit outside at **Café Cappuccino**. The garden is screened by the red-brick arcade of **Basarhallene**, a semi-circular wall of little shops, galleries, and cafés; some, such as the **Café Bacchus**, are open until at least 1am (except on Sunday).

Back along Karl Johans Gate, the **Storting**, built in the 1860s, looks over the small park of **Løvebakken** (the Lion's Hill) to the **National Theatre** and, with perhaps unconscious symbolism, up towards the Royal Palace. When the Storting is sitting, the public galleries are open to the public. Between mid to late June and the end of September, when the government is in recess, there are daily tours at 11am, noon, and 1pm, led by a guide who explains the parliamentary system simply and shows you the two main debating chambers, the **Odelsting** and the **Lagting**.

Between the Storting and the National Theatre is Studenterlunden, the Students' Park, situated opposite the main university building. The Great Hall of the University, with its celebrated murals by Edvard Munch, is unfortunately no longer open to the public except for concerts and other special events.

The National Theatre is a beautiful building, the heart of Oslo's theatre life. In the surrounding garden are statues of the writers Henrik Ibsen and Bjørnstjere Bjørnson. To Oslonians, the National Theatre is Ibsen's theatre. (Ask at the Tourist Information Centre about plans for a special Ibsen tour to include the theatre and his

Oslo University

Steel and glass at Aker Brygge

Oslo flat near the Royal Palace which was converted into a small museum. This was where he lived from 1895–1906 and it has been restored to its previous ambience, with changing and permanent exhibitions. Arbiensgate 1; tel: 22-55-20-09; open Tuesday to Sunday 12–3pm; guided English-language tours at 12pm, 1pm and 2pm.) Almost all National Theatre plays are presented in Norwegian, except during the September **Ibsen Festival**, when foreign companies perform in their own languages. At other times it is still be worth visiting for the magnificence of the auditorium. The theatre houses a rare collection of portraits of famous artists and dramatists by well-known Norwegian painters such as Munch, Krohg, Werenskiold, and Sørensen.

A rest and a chat

Ahead is the **Royal Palace** (Slottet), with parks on either side open to the public. The palace itself, with a dominating statue of King Karl Johan in front, is not open but the **Changing the Guard** takes place daily at 1.30pm. On Saturday the Royal Guard, accompanied by the Royal Band, begins its march from the Akerhus Castle at 12.45pm, en-route to the Royal Palace.

There are two choices for a quick lunch before the Fjord Cruise. Either try one of the cafés and restaurants along Karl Johans Gate, such as the popular Sara's Telt – the open-air cafe on Studenterlunden – or turn down Roald Amundsen's Gate or Rosenkrantz Gate, to the glass and steel of **Aker Brygge**, facing the sea on the right of the City Hall. Built on to the wharf-houses that once lined the quay, two of which still stand, Aker Brygge is a modern enclosed shopping complex that on a sunny summer day makes a fine place for lunch beside the water, although it is very tourist oriented. The heart is **Festplassen**, which faces the marina. If it is too cold outside, you can see it all through wide glass windows. The choice of lunch is huge, ranging from a sandwich and a beer to a more full meal.

Better yet, for real harbour ambience and excellent seafood specialities, go down to the harbour to Pier 34 for **Solsiden Oyster Bar/Restaurant** at 34 Søndre Akershuskai (open only in spring and summer, tel: 22-33-36-30). Make sure to finish lunch in time to reach **Pier 3** on the quay in front of the City Hall, from where the boat leaves around 10.30am, 1pm and 3.30pm (check at the Tourist Office or in the *Oslo Guide* for exact times; book through Båtservice Sightseeing, tel: 22-20-07-15). This two-hour **Fjord Cruise** sweeps out through the harbour, where ferries, cruise boats and yachts attest to Norway's long-standing preoccupation with the sea. In spring and summer you can buy fresh shrimp from a fishing boat on the landing to eat while strolling – an Oslo tradition.

As the boat heads out, on the peninsula to the left is Akershus, a medieval fortress still in use by the military. Look behind to the hill and forest rising behind central Oslo and the white scoop of the **Holmenkollen Ski Jump** (Holmenkollenbakken). For the next couple of hours, the boat weaves through islands and narrow sounds. This cruise service runs from May through late September. A **50-minute mini-cruise** also leaves on the hour and is free to Oslo card holders. (Check at the office for departure times. Check in 15 minutes before departure.) There are various lunch and evening buffet cruises, when you may go ashore to eat, or tackle prawns on board.

Sara's Telt café in central Oslo

The Storting

Have dinner at one of Oslo's newest seafood restaurants, **Wollans**, Rådhusgata 28, tel: 22-41-19-14). Wollans serves a wide range of fresh fish and seafood dishes, made with regional and seasonal ingredients. A two-course meal should cost in the region of 330NKR per person.

After eating, wander off in search of some music to **Smuget** (tel: 22-42-52-62), whose nightly programme ranges from jazz to blues and rock, fortunately on different floors, and stays open until 4am, closed Sunday. To find it at Rosenkrantzgate 22, turn left off Karl Johans Gate, near the Domkirke, and go through the courtyard. An alternative is the **Odeon**, at Hedgehaugsveien 34 (tel: 22-69-05-35) in the Frogner quarter, which features different music each night in a lively complex that includes a bar, restaurant and popular summer terrace.

2. Historic Oslo

A walk through Christiania (old Oslo) towards the Akershus Castle. Lunch at the Engebret Café, followed by an afternoon in the Museum of Contemporary Art. In the evening, a concert at Konserthus followed by dinner in Gamle Raadhuset.

Christiania, named after that great builder-king Christian IV of Denmark and Norway, came into being in 1624, when the medieval city of Oslo, across the bay below Ekeberg Hill, burnt down. Christian designed what he hoped would be a fire-proof city with roads 15m (49ft) wide, laid in a grid pattern with buildings of stone or half-timber only. It says a lot for Christian's skill as a planner that the road system still forms the heart of central Oslo, though few of the original buildings remain.

From a starting point at Jernbanetorget, turn left into Fred Olsens Gate and walk along past **Børsen**, the old Stock Exchange. Still in use today, it was designed in the 1820s by the architect Christian H Grosch, who was also responsible for planning much of the expanded city. Not far away in Myntgate, **Den Gamle Logen**, which has been used for festive occasions for the last 150 years, is once again a concert hall.

The city's careful design is made even clearer when you see the **Christiania Bymodell**, situated under the walls of Akershus Castle (Slott). To reach it, turn right into **Rådhusgate** past No 19, a restaurant and art gallery to which we will be returning later, left into Kongensgate past Bankplassen, where you will be lunching, and right into Myntgate. Continue until you come to the long, low building known as **Høymagasinet** (Hay Barn), which houses the Bymodell. This model of Christiania as it looked in 1838 spreads over an area of 10 x 15m (33 x 49ft), which gives a three-dimensional

The Stock Exchange

view of the city. This model is part of a multi-media programme, shown on a 24m² (258 ft²) free-hanging screen and featuring a 20-minute screen presentation that traces Christiania's development from 1624–1840. Guided tours are given in English.

Look closely and, opposite Raadmannsgården, you will find **Gamle Raadhuset** (the Old City Hall; tel: 22-42-01-07) at Nedre Slottsgate 1, another of the oldest buildings in Oslo.

Just a few steps on from Høymagasinet, turn into **Kirkegate** and the main entrance to Akershus Castle. At the lower end beside the parade ground and the Armed Forces Museum is a monument to the victims of World War II. A gigantic woman and a small man in the circle of the earth symbolise his death and her continuing life and struggle. The sculptor was Gunnar Jansson. The **Armed Forces Museum** (Forsvarsmuseet; tel: 23-09-35-82) nearby houses the Buick in which Crown Prince Olav (later King Olav) toured Oslo on his triumphant return after World War II, and some of the tiny aircraft that struggled so bravely against insuperable odds. It also has the only cafeteria in the area.

The first castle at **Akershus**, with a big central tower, was built around AD1300 by Håkon V Magnusson, and commands the whole

The Akershus stronghold

of the bay and fjord. In the early 17th century, Christian IV rebuilt the fortress as a royal castle and, thanks to restoration early in the 20th century, much of the fortification looks today as it must have done back then. Inside there is a long courtyard with a tower at each end, and **Olav's Hall** (tel: 22-41-25-21), used as a prison in World War II for members of the Norwegian Resistance. The castle is also a royal mausoleum, with the tombs of King Haakon VII, Queen Maud and Crown Princess Martha, alongside those of Sigurd Jorsalfarer and Håkon V Magnusson, the builder.

The **Resistance Museum** (Norges Hjemmefrontmuseet; tel: 23-09-31-38) is in a part of the castle known as the **Double Battery** and the **Frame House**. It is effectively laid out, starting with cuttings from the September 1938 meeting between Neville Chamberlain, the British Prime Minister, and Hitler in Munich and ends with pictures of the joyous liberation. Between are records of heroism and touchingly simple personal accounts. The museum stands next to the memorial to the 42 Resistance members who were executed there. At the end of World War II, for a short period Norway restored the death penalty. The traitor Vidkun Quisling was sentenced to death and shot at Akershus.

Lunch at **Engebret Café** (tel: 22-33-66-94) on Bankplassen 1, a restaurant as old as the district itself, can be inside or outdoor, large or small – a tempting *smørbrød* between 11am and 3pm (from 3–10.30pm the restaurant is *à la carte*). The food is good and this is a popular spot for local business people to entertain.

Across the square is the **National Museum of Contemporary Art** (Museet for Samtidskunst; tel: 22-86-22-10), opened in 1990 in what was formerly the Bank of Norway's headquarters.The museum now holds all the post-war collections transferred from the National Gallery and Norway's State Travelling Gallery. Probably the best known internationally of the contemporary painters exhibited are Jacob Weideman and Anna-Eva Bornman. Of them all, Arne Ekeland is widely considered to be the most important painter. The museum's principal sculptors are Arnold Haukeland, Knut Steen, and Nils Aas. (You can also see sculptures

Colourful traditional costumes

by both Haukeland and Aas in Bergen on Ventre Stromkai and in the Teaterparken.)

An interesting selection of contemporary art is on display at the **Astrup Fearnley Museum**, in a unique building at Grev Wedels pl. 9, tel: 22-93-60-60. Just nearby is the Norwegian Museum of Architecture, at Kongensgate 4, tel: 22-42-40-80, which has a permanent exhibition of Norwegian architecture of the past 1000 years. The cafe is a meeting place for local artists and designers.

My suggestion for your evening is to go to Oslo's **Konserthus**, (Concert Hall; tel: 23-11-31-00), home of the Oslo Philharmonic, in residence from early September to June each year; pop concerts are also hosted here. **Den Gamle Logen** (tel: 22-33-44-70), **Akershus Castle** (tel: 22-41-25-21) and the **University Aula** (tel: 22-85-97-11), among others, also have classical music performances in the summer, which usually start around 7.30pm. Summer is the time for festivals of all sorts, from opera and chamber music to theatre and jazz. Even if you are not a folklore addict, sample the music and costumes of Norwegian folklore in the small auditorium of the Konserthus on Mondays and Thursdays in July and most of August.

For dinner, **Gamle Raadhuset** (the Old City Hall) is one of the oldest houses in Christiania which, in the past, has done duty as courtroom and dungeon, assembly rooms, concert hall and even as a place for church services. In 1856 it was sold to Matheus Helseth who opened it as a restaurant. Today, the present owners have done much to restore the building, with a restaurant in the former wine cellars. It is well known for its seafood; a two-course meal will cost between 300–380NKR per person, without wine.

Afterwards, cross the road to try **Kafé Celsius** (tel: 22-42-45-39), as much for the building as the coffee, for this is Rådhusgate 19, the oldest surviving house in Christiania. Kafé Celsius attracts an artistic, literary crowd and is open until 1am.

3. Bygdøy Day

Ferry or bus to the island of Bygdøy to see the Norwegian Folk Museum and Viking Ship Museum. Lunch at the Najaden Restaurant in the Sjøfartsmuseum (Maritime Museum). On to the Kon Tiki and Ra Museum. Finally to the Fram Museum before taking the boat or bus back. Dinner at a choice of fine restaurants, followed by a visit to a nightclub.

The Bygdøy ferry leaves from Pier 3 in front of the Rådhuset (same pier as *Itinerary 1*) and you get off at **Dronningen**, the boat's first stop on Bygdøy. (By bus, take the No 30, marked Bygdøy, from the National Theatre and ask for the Folk Museum.) Once off the boat, take note of **Lanternen Kro** (Huk Aveny 2, tel: 22-43-81-25) a traditional old inn, as a possible lunch alternative to **Najaden** (Bygdøynesveien 7, tel: 22-43-81-80), though it will mean returning to this point after the museum tours.

Walk up the hill (Huk Aveny) to a turning on the right, well signed for the **Norwegian Folk Museum** (tel: 22-12-37-00). Scandinavians love their outdoor folk museums, large collections of buildings showing a way of life that lasted longer here than in many other parts of Europe. This one was founded in 1894 when, in areas such as Setesdal, the way of life depicted was only just

Traditional house in the Folk Museum

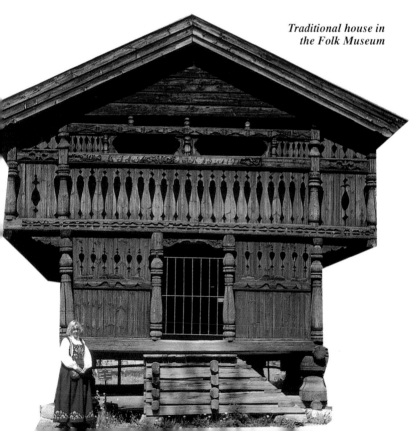

The Norwegian Folk Museum

beginning to change. This brings a rare authenticity to the 170 old buildings from more than 20 different areas of Norway.

Norway's vast distances meant that farms were scattered, and there were few villages with a large number of houses. A group of buildings in the museum will usually turn out to be the component parts – store, kitchen, *stua* (living room), loft – of one farm. These beautiful, dark wooden buildings with their carved exterior galleries and stairs, are not only from rural areas. There is a waiting room for steamship passengers from Pipervika in Oslo, old mills, and a stave church from 1200.

Return to the main road, turn right and the **Viking Ship Museum** (Vikingskipshuset; tel: 22-43-83-79) is only a short and pleasant walk. The three longships found in the Oslofjord area all ended their careers as burial ships and contained a wealth of the household implements, jewellery and weaponry that the Vikings considered necessary in the afterlife. They are the Tune ship, found 1867, the Gokstad ship, excavated 1880, and the Oseberg ship, which were discovered in 1904; probably the oldest of the three, it was built around AD800.

The Gokstad ship was the best preserved, complete with the skeleton of its royal chief. The ship was built of oak, is 24m (80ft) long, and was originally designed for sailing and fighting. The

Folk-dancing

Oseberg ship, slightly smaller but with a burial chamber luxurious enough to indicate royalty, held skeletons of two women. This may have been the grave of Queen Åsa, the only known queen in the early Yngling dynasty, and her bondswoman. A modern replica of the Gokstad ship recently made a successful crossing to New York. According to the ancient Sagas, whose statements are now backed by modern archaeology, the Vikings made the same voyage almost 1,000 years before when Leif Eriksson discovered Vinland den Gode (the land of good pasture) his name for North America, in a foray from Greenland in AD1000.

The walk down to **Bygdøynes** is quite a hike but has the bonus that you can call in and look at the old **Sjømanskirke**, facing the sea. This is rarely open but if you ring the bell the custodian will almost certainly let you have a look. The alternative, once again, is bus No 30 from the Viking ships to Bygdøynes.

At Bygdøynes, the ferry terminal, the first things you notice are the fore-and-aft schooner *Svanen*, not just part of the museum but a floating centre set up every summer for youth clubs and school children; and the polar vessel *Gjøa*, once a seal-hunter. *Gjøa* was Roald Amundsen's vessel for his epic journey through the Northwest Passage. Having departed in 1903, it took until August 1906 to navigate a way through – a journey which provided excellent preparation for Amundsen's meticulously planned and successful attempt on the South Pole when, by just a month, he beat the British team led by Captain Scott. Before tackling the museums proper, there is time for lunch at **Najaden**, part of the **Norsk Sjøfartsmuseum** (Maritime Museum; tel: 22-43-82-40), where you will find Norwegian specialities and a good cold buffet table.

The sea and the long coast have been a constant link in Norway's social history and the Maritime Museum aims to show much of it, from the model of the Kvaldor boat, a dugout from AD600, to a vessel of the mid-19th century (*Kong Sverre* built at Horten), and finally to a modern tanker. *Kong Sverre* displaced 3,500 tons and was the largest and most powerfully armed wooden warship built in Scandinavia. The Boat Hall, in a separate building opposite the main entrance houses many of the small boats that were as characteristic of their districts as the distinctive regional wooden houses and

The Viking Ship Museum

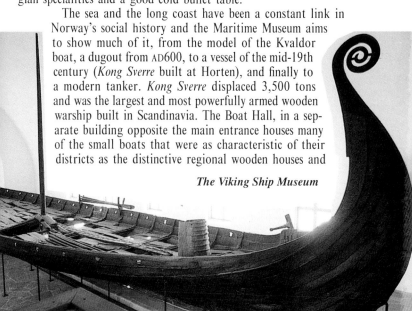

The Fram caught in pack ice

national costumes in the Folk Museum. Closer to the ferry is the **Kon-Tiki Museum** (tel: 22-43-80-50) and Fridtjof Nansen's polar ship *Fram*. I always leave the **Fram Museum** (tel: 22-43-83-70) to last because, of all maritime museums, it is the most atmospheric.

In 1947, Thor Heyerdahl's feat in building a balsa raft, the *Kon-Tiki*, and sailing it across the Pacific grabbed the imagination of the world. Many still come to see the raft, which is well displayed on two floors. Part of the same building holds *Ra II*, Heyerdahl's second craft, a reed boat built in Egypt at the foot of the Giza pyramids and used to test a theory that this sort of boat could have reached the West Indies long before Columbus.

The *Fram* made three remarkable voyages through the ice and yet there she stands, sturdy and trim and freshly painted, in the museum specially built for her in 1935. Round the walls of the hall are artefacts and documents from the ship's remarkable history. Her first voyage was disastrous: three years spent stuck in pack ice. Otto Sverdrup led *Fram's* second expedition to the islands north of Arctic Canada, and in 1910, Amundsen took the ship south for his onslaught on the South Pole.

As you climb the gangway it hardly seems possible that this spick and span ship could ever have been covered in cobwebs of frost

Ra II goes to sea

A statue guards the Theatercaféen

and endured the pressure of the 'ice-quakes'. Today, she is scrubbed and polished with cabins and their contents still intact. Before you leave Bygdøynes, walk down to the point to see **Joseph Grimeland's memorial** to the 4,500 Norwegian sailors who perished during World War II. Near it is the **Mine Box**, a monument to the 2,100 Norwegian merchant seamen who lost their lives in World War I.

Dinner at **Theatercaféen** or the **Grand Café** has atmosphere whichever one you chose. Theatercaféen (tel: 22-33-32-00), in the Hotel Continental across Stortings Gata from the National Theatre, opened its doors in 1900; it is especially known for its glassed-in verandah over the street, open from spring to late autumn. On a Friday or Saturday night it is wise to book. The place is famous as a haunt of actors, artists and the intelligentsia and the walls are studded with portraits and pencil sketches of many of Norway's leading artists, past and present. The food is commendably straightforward and versatile, and the service is excellent.

The Grand Café (tel: 22-42-93-90) in the Grand Hotel on Karl Johans Gate was a haunt of Oslo's 19th-century Bohemians. On the far wall is a huge mural painted by **Per Krohg**, showing a gathering of admirers as Ibsen arrives for lunch. The menu includes some Norwegian specialities and this could be the place to try reindeer, which is a bit like roast beef and very tender.

Nightclubs open and close with great frequency in Oslo and it is always risky to recommend other than the most established. If you like jazz, you will not go wrong with **Stortorvets Gjaestgiveri**, a traditional cafe/restaurant that features live jazz most nights, Grensen 1 (tel: 22-42-88-63). **Herr Nilsen**, at C.J. Hambros Plass 5 (tel: 22-33-54-05), is another popular jazz bar. It is centrally located and plays host to a variety of jazz, from mainstream to bebop.

A day in the open air of the Nordmarka – forest, hill and lake – to see Tryvannstårnet, Holmenkollen and the ski jump.

The whole of central Oslo is surrounded by an area of forest, lakes, hills and moor known as the Marka. It is ideal for winter skiing, summer walking, canoeing and fishing – particularly the accessible Nordmarka, which is dotted with *markastuer*: places where you can eat, rest and, in some cases, find accommodation.

Cross-country skiing is a national winter sport and on Sundays whole families are out in the Marka with tiny babies securely wrapped behind the windshields of their *pulker* (little sledges). In summer, you

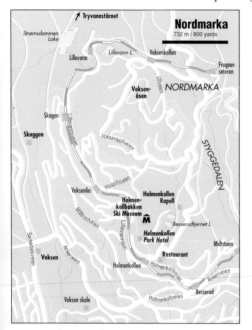

can combine walking with stops at Tryvannstårnet and the Holmenkollen ski jump. Take T-bane train No 15 from **Stortinget** underground station to **Frognerseteren**, from where a network of clearly marked paths leads out into the Nordmarka. The one for **Tryvannstårnet** takes around 15–20 minutes. The drive from central Oslo to the top takes around the same time but the walk is part of the day's outing.

Tryvannstårnet is not only Oslo's radio and telephone tower, but it also affords the best view in Southern Norway. Take the lift which rises nearly 118m (387ft) in a surging 11 seconds. From the observation platform, you are nearly 588m (1,929ft) above sea level and the view is magnificent. On a good day, it covers around 30,000km^2 (18,000 square miles) and over to the east you can see as far as Sweden. South is Oslo and the fjord islands and in every other direction stretches of open land and forests seem to go on forever.

The easiest way to go down to **Holmenkollen** is to follow the road to **Voksenkollen** station to the corner where it meets Holmenkollveien. Looking towards the great ski jump you will see the pool area which is used in summer for concerts. The alternative way down is longer. If you feel daring and want to experience how it feels to set off on one of the world's toughest downhill runs, try the popular ski simulator, complete with eye-view film which creates a realistic experience. Follow the track signed Frognerseteren past **Øvresetertjern** lake and down through the forest to the 100-year-

old **Frognerseteren Restaurant** (tel: 22-14-05-50), which offers an excellent *koldtbord*, the traditional lavish cold buffet table. There are wooden tables outside where people take their own picnics. From here, take the marked forest route to the left of the main road down to Holmenkollen until the track crosses the road just above **Holmenkollen Kapell.**

The **Holmenkollen Ski Jumping Competition**, which is held in March each year, started in 1892 and is the oldest in the world. The last day has the Great Ski Jump when the crowd is so huge that it seems Oslo must be empty. To get a feel for the jump (but only if you like heights) go first to the top of the jumping tower. Tickets are on sale next door in the **Ski Museum** (tel: 22-92-32-00). There is a lift but the last stairway before the top is a steep climb.

The Ski Museum's earliest relic is a copy of the 4,000-year-old rock carving of a skier from Rødøy in Nordland. The exhibition ranges over the development of skiing in Norway. There are tableaux of Amundsen's and Nansen's expeditions, a history of royal skiing and is a tribute to **Sondre Norheim**, the father of modern skiing.

Holmenkollen Restaurant (tel: 22-14-62-26), near the Museum, has wonderful views and serves good Norwegian dishes. The nearby Holmenkollen Cafeteria sells *smørbrød* (open sandwiches). The walk down to the Holmenkollen station takes 10 minutes, and within half an hour you are back in the city.

Norwegians are passionate skiers

5. Vigeland and the By Museum

A morning's visit, to the Frogner park (not to be confused with Frognerseteren), the Vigeland Museum and the nearby Oslo Bymuseum (City Museum).

Go first to **Frogner**, a lovely neighbourhood on the fashionable west side of the city. The ambience here is lively, and there are cafes and fashion boutiques along streets such as Bygdøy Allé, Frognerveien and Kirkeveien, which leads to the Majorstuen Quarter, another vibrant neighbourhood, dotted with antiques shops and cafés.

Frogner holds the bulk of the masterpieces by the sculptor Gustav **Vigeland** (1869–1943): five great groups of figures, linked together along an axis over 850m (930yds) long. Vigeland held his first independent exhibition in 1894, when he was only 25. He was a good negotiator and in 1921 struck a deal with the City of Oslo by which he donated all his works of art in return for a studio – his studio is now the **Vigeland Museum** *(see right)*.

Take a tram 12 or 15 and ask for the Vigeland Park main entrance. Through these big gates, the path runs up to a bridge, lined with 58 bronze statues of human figures. From the left-hand side of the bridge can be seen a carved circle of children in relaxed poses. The bridge leads to the great bowl of the fountain, held up by six male figures and surrounded by a mosaic of black and white granite. Beyond and above is **Monoliten** (the Monolith) Vigeland's most famous work. Carved in granite from a single stone it depicts human figures, groping towards the sky. The Monolith is the centrepiece of a hill, encircled by tiers of steps with 12 groups of figures on them, showing the cycle of life from childhood to death.

The park's final sculpture is the Wheel of Life, a group of seven colossal figures.

On the way to the Vigeland Museum, just outside the park and across **Halvdan Svartes Gate**, call in at the **Oslo Bymuseum** (tel: 22-43-06-45), Oslo's city museum which lies in the lovely old Frogner Manor (Frognerveien 67) and has one of the largest collections of paintings in Norway. The main building, dating from 1790, shows city interiors and paintings; other exhibits round the courtyard are based on themes such as town planning and trade, illustrating how recently Norway became a modern industrialised country. The museum has a photograph of the finest building in the so-called 'English quarter', just past the **Royal Park** on **Drammenveien**, where Oslo's first examples of late French Renaissance style rose in the 1880s. The building has been replaced by a 1960s block, in front of which is a statue of Winston Churchill.

On the way back to the town centre, look out for the statue on your right-hand side just after the two main roads join. A little further into the centre is the Nobel

The monolith in Vigeland park

38

High flying in the park

Building, where the winner of the Peace Prize is decided. Though Nobel was a Swede, the countries were still united at the turn of the 20th century when he inaugurated the scheme and decreed that Norway should award the Prize.

Finally, call in at the **Vigeland Museum**, Nobels gate 32 (tel: 22-44-11-36). The museum and park (the latter is open 24 hours) house nearly all Vigeland's powerful, sensual works including over 2,000 sculptures, drawings and wood cuts. On summer evenings, there are sometimes concerts in the courtyard, and the terrace overlooking the park is a lovely spot to have lunch or a cup of tea (museum open May–September, Tuesday–Saturday 10am–6pm, Sunday noon–7pm; October–April, Thursday–Saturday noon–4pm, Sunday noon–6pm). During the winter months the park is used for cross-country skiing.

6. The Munch Museum and Botanic Garden

An afternoon's visit to see the enormous collection of the works of Norway's greatest painter, and the Botanic Garden.

To reach the **Munch Museum** (June–early September, daily 10am–6pm; mid-September–May, Tuesday–Sunday 10am–4pm, Thursday and Sunday until 6pm; tel: 22-67-37-74) at Tøyen, take bus No 20 from Jernbanetorget or the T-bane (underground) trains No 1,2,3,4 or 5 from Stortinget to Tøyen. The museum lies opposite Tøyenhagen, which houses the **Oslo Botanic Garden**.

Munch self-portrait

Munch and Vigeland were almost the same age. They became friends in Berlin and remained so until they both fell in love with the same woman, Dagny Juel, also a painter. Munch despised Vigeland's bargain with the City of Oslo *(see Itinerary 5)* and donated all his own work to Oslo on his death in 1944. It includes 1,100 paintings and 18,000 prints as well as 4,500 drawings, plates, and many letters, so much material that the exhibition is constantly changing. Munch returned to the same themes in different forms, so that a painting you come across in the National Gallery may be similar but not identical to one on display in the Munch Museum.

Munch's background, unlike that of Vigeland, was comfortable and intellectual; his father was a doctor, and his uncle one of the leading historians of his age. However, his mother died early, and something of his father's gloomy nature communicated itself to the boy. One of Munch's most famous subjects, *The Sick Child*, was inspired by his sister's death. Munch started as a Naturalist and, after a short period as an Impressionist, he became recognised as a strong pioneering influence on Expressionism across Europe. After a mental breakdown early in the 20th century, he moved to landscape painting; as he recovered, he gradually returned to Expressionism. This period, around 1916, saw the completion of his great murals for the University Aula, and his sketches for *The Sun* and *Alma Mater* also date from the years after his illness.

Best known of his earlier works is his *Life Cycle: Puberty*, *The Kiss*, *Anxiety*, *Melancholy*, *Death in the Sickroom* and *The Sick Child*. Some are in the museum, others were sold during his lifetime. Very striking is the *Death of Marat*.

The Museum restaurant serves traditional Norwegian dishes which you could sample before a visit to the oasis of the **Botanic Gardens**, which close at 8pm in summer, and **Museum**. The gardens have beautiful, exotic species and more than 1,000 mountain plants. The lower level of the museum has an historical overview of Munch's interesting life with photographs, drawings and documents.

If you want to devote a day to this Munch/Botanic Gardens visit, you could reverse the order and visit Tøyenhagen in the morning and include the **Zoological**, and **Mineral and Geological museums**, both in the same gardens but closed by 4pm Tuesday–Sunday. The Munch Museum stays open until 6pm in summer.

Rest after exhausting sight-seeing

7. Art and Museums

The National Gallery (Nasjonalgalleriet), Oslo Rådhus (City Hall), the Historical Museum (Tulinløkka) and the Museum of Applied Art (Kunstindustrimuseet). Note: on Monday, when most museums are closed, a good alternative to the museums listed here is the Henie Onstad Kunstsenter (tel: 67-54-30-50), housing the modern art collection of the international skating champion Sonja Henie and her husband, Niels Onstad. The centre is in the suburb of Høvikodden, about an hour's bus ride out of the centre of Oslo (bus Nos 151, 153, 161, 162, 251 or 261).

All these museums are within easy walking distance of Karl Johans Gate. Start with the **National Gallery** (opens at 10am; closed Tuesday; guided tours Monday and Wednesday–Friday 10am, 12pm and 2pm), home to the state's largest collection of paintings, sculptures and graphic art. This is the place to trace the great surge of 19th-century Norwegian painting, prompted mainly by feelings of nationalism. The Norwegian contribution to the National Romantic movement was typified by painters such as Adolph Tidemand and Hans Gude; their picture *Brudeferd i Hardanger* (Bridal Voyage on the Hardanger Fjord) may now seem over-theatrical, but its four versions were hugely popular when first painted. There is also a whole room devoted to Edvard Munch, which includes *The Scream and t*he gallery also has a fine European collection by masters such as Rubens, El Greco, Cézanne, Degas, Braque and Picasso.

An ice cream in the morning...

The Historical Museum

Oslo Rådhus (City Hall) was planned in 1915 and begun in the 1930s. It is an odd mixture of romanticism, classicism and functionalism, but the front steps in Fridtjof Nansens Plass are impressive. On the sides of the courtyard is the **Yggdrasil Frieze**, depicting themes from Norse mythology.

It is just short walk up from Fridtjof Nansens Plass back to Karl Johans Gate and towards the Palace. Turn right into Frederiksgate and head for the **Historical Museum**, part of the University. It consists of three departments: the **Ethnographic Museum**, the **Numismatic Collection** and the **Collection of Antiquities**. The **Viking Hall** gives the background to the discovery of the three ships that are now on display at Bygdøy; the Treasury houses gold and silver wares; the Middle Ages collection predates the paintings in the National Gallery and is Oslo's richest collection of art up to 1530. Step across Halfdan Kjerulfs Plass and onto St Olavs Gate to reach the **Museum of Applied Art** (Kunstindustrimuseet; tel: 22-20-35-78; Tuesday–Friday 11am–3pm, Saturday–Sunday noon–4pm, Thursday evening until 7pm), housing the 13th-century Baldishol Tapestry. Another notable museum option, near the Oslo Concert Hall, is the **Stenersen Museum**, with permanent and changing exhibitions of Norwegian art from 1850–1970 (Munkedamsveien 15, tel: 22-83-95-60).

8. Afternoon Shopping

Shopping under a glass roof has its benefits in a northern climate; Oslo has plunged into shopping centres in a big way whilst preserving its traditional specialist shops.

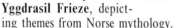

The biggest shopping centre in Oslo, located at Stenersgate, is **Oslo City**, an overwhelming colossus of glass and white marble, where shops stay open until 8pm during the week and 6pm on Saturday. **Aker Brygge** down by the harbour is similar but places greater emphasis on eating, drinking and entertainment. **Paleet**, which opens on to Karl Johans Gate, opposite Studenterlunden, is one of the most elegant centres. Many people, however, find it preferable to browse along city streets searching out the specialist shops or to wander the shopping streets in the Frogner and Majorstuen neighbourhoods.

Aker Brygge shopping centre

Nostalgic settlement of accounts

Oslo's biggest and most comprehensive department store is **Steen & Strøm** (Kongensgate 23), near the Jernbanetorget end of Karl Johans gate. **Glas Magasinet** in Stortorvet promotes high-quality Norwegian glass, china and pewter. The ground-floor tourist shop sells ceramics and other craft work and hand-knitted Norwegian sweaters.

Norwegian chocolate is a dream. **Freia** is one of the best-known makes, and the company has a shop in Karl Johans gate. **David Andersen** jewellery is among the best known in Norway and also has its own shop (Karl Johans gate 20). **Donna's Smykkegalleri Basarhallene**, Stotetorvet 1B has a lovely selection of Norwegian silver, gold, and precious stones. **Porsgrund at** Karl Johans gate 14 offers fine porcelain

Grensen and **Lille Grensen** are happy hunting grounds for bargains, particularly at the latter's outdoor stalls, and **Youngstorget**, as well as **Stortorvet**, has a daily flower market. There is a flea market every Saturday during summer on **Vestkanttorget** by Frogner Park, and on weekends at Youngstorget and a flower market in front of the Cathedral. For antiques, try the best, biggest and most expensive, **Kaare Berntsen** in Universitetsgaten 12, opposite the National Gallery. There is also a large number of antiques shops in the Majorstuen and Frogner quarters, along the Industrigata and Hedgehaugsveien. **Husfliden**, Rosenkrantzgaten 8, is the largest stockist of Norwegian craftwork, from furniture to toys and *bunader* (national costumes).

Modern architecture at Aker Brygge

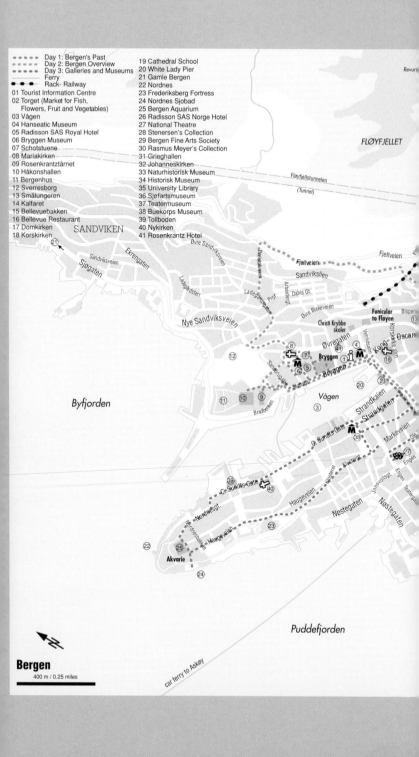

Day 1: Bergen's Past
Day 2: Bergen Overview
Day 3: Galleries and Museums
Ferry
Rack- Railway

01 Tourist Information Centre
02 Torget (Market for Fish,
   Flowers, Fruit and Vegetables)
03 Vågen
04 Hanseatic Museum
05 Radisson SAS Royal Hotel
06 Bryggen Museum
07 Schotstuene
08 Mariakirken
09 Rosenkrantztårnet
10 Håkonshallen
11 Bergenhus
12 Sverresborg
13 Smålungeren
14 Kalfaret
15 Bellevuebakken
16 Bellevue Restaurant
17 Domkirken
18 Korskirken

19 Cathedral School
20 White Lady Pier
21 Gamle Bergen
22 Nordnes
23 Frederiksberg Fortress
24 Nordnes Sjobad
25 Bergen Aquarium
26 Radisson SAS Norge Hotel
27 National Theatre
28 Stenersen's Collection
29 Bergen Fine Arts Society
30 Rasmus Meyer's Collection
31 Grieghallen
32 Johanneskirken
33 Naturhistorisk Museum
34 Historisk Museum
35 University Library
36 Sjøfartsmuseum
37 Teatermuseum
38 Buekorps Museum
39 Tollboden
40 Nykirken
41 Rosenkrantz Hotel

FLØYFJELLET

Fløyfjellstunnelen
(Tunnel)

Revuri

SANDVIKEN

Byfjorden

Sjøgaten
Sandviksveien
Ekrengaten

Øvre Sandviksveien
Fjellveien
Fjellveien
Sandvikslien
Ladegårdsgaten
Prof. Dahls Gt.
Arbeidergt.
Øvre Blekeveien
Nye Sandviksveien

Funicular
to Floyen

Bispene

Christi Krybbe
skoler
Øvregaten
Vetrlidsalm
Kong Oscars
Oscars
Korskirke alm

(8)
(7)
(41)
M
(4)
M
(18)

M
(5)
Bryggen
Bryggen

(6)

(12)

(11)
(10)
(9)
Bradbenken
Skuteviken
Sandviksveien

Vågen

(3)

Strandkaien
Strandgaten
Strandkaien

G. Sundts Gate
M
(38)
Markeveien

(26)
(27)

C. Sundts Gate
(39)
(40)

Nordnesgt.
Nordnesbakken - Haugeveien
Haugeveien
Klostergt.
Klostergt.

(23)

Nøstegaten
Nøstegaten
Jonsvollgt.
Engen
Engen
Teatergt.

(22)
(25)
Akvarie

(24)

Puddefjorden

N

Bergen
400 m / 0.25 miles

car ferry to Askoy

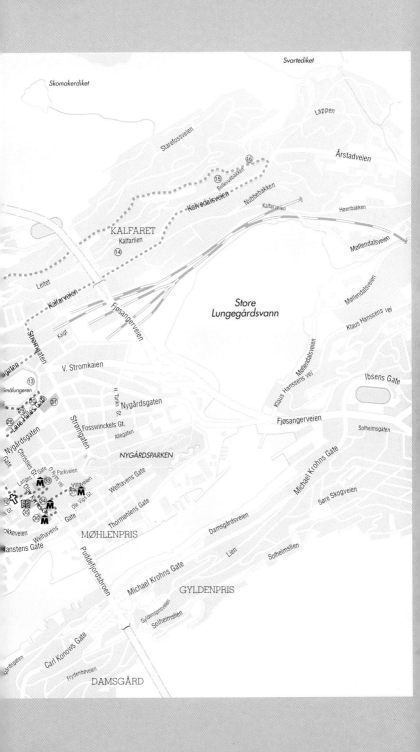

BERGEN I[...]

The heart of Bergen is Torget, the harbour square, where King Olav Kyrre founded his city in the 11th century. Today a daily fish, flower and fruit market is held here. Along the wharf, huddling close to the castle for protection, the medieval town grew and became the first capital of a united Norway and its biggest city until the 20th century when it was overtaken by Oslo. Bergen today has the natural layout and charm of a community built on hills. Almost all the itineraries on the following pages are based on public transport or walking – make sure you have a comfortable pair of shoes for an energetic day. Bergen's rain is a national (though not necessarily always justified) joke and it has to be said that, when it does rain, the skies empty.

Bergen Tourist Board produces the invaluable *Bergen Guide*. I have found *Round Bergen on Foot* and *Skulpturer i Bergen* (Sculpture in Bergen), which describes some of the city's many sculptures, add interest to exploring. Another good book available at the Tourist Office is *Bergen: A Cultural Guide* by Norvall Skreien. Museums are mostly closed on Monday, and shut their doors at 3 or 4pm in the summer months (earlier in winter). Ask also about the Bergen Card, which provides visitors with free admission to most museums, the funicular and central swimming baths and includes free bus travel in central Bergen, as well as offering discounts on some attractions. Price is 150NKR for 24 hours, 230NKR for 48 hours.

9. Bergen's Past

From the Vågen fish market to Bryggen, the old part of the city, the Bryggen museums and the Mariakirken. To Fiskekrogen for lunch. In the afternoon to Rosenkrantztårnet and Håkonshallen Bergen's castles. Dinner at Enhjøringen on Bryggen.

On the way to **Vågen**, the old harbour at the edge of **Torget** with its fish, flower and fruit market, make time to visit the **Tourist Information Office** (tel: 55-32-14-80; www.visitbergen.com); this is located opposite the harbour and the fish market, on Vågsallmenningen square, by the Holberg statue.

Bergen's fish market is awake early, and popular with locals and visitors alike. It dates back to the 16th century and today flowers

What's on offer at the fish market

Old merchant's house in Bergen

and fruit are sold here, as well as fish. You can buy smoked salmon or shrimp rolls and the perenially popular fish cakes relatively cheaply and keep them for a snack lunch; neat salmon packages that are easy to take home at the end of your visit are also available here. Notice the three flag poles guarded by stone lions which mark out a triangle that was once a ceremonial quay. A little further out is the fine sailing ship *Statsraad Lehmkuhl*, now a sail training ship, also hired out for special occasions. On the right towards the sea, note **Zachariasbryggen**, an old warehouse, now largely reconstructed, with shops, restaurants, cafés and a service centre for visitors travelling by boat. The warehouse is the site of Fiskekrogen (tel: 55-55-96-40), which has tables outside in summer and is your target for a light lunch.

Bryggen, on the east side of Vågen, is the oldest part of the city, where a line of medieval houses once clustered close to the water. King Olav Kyrre founded Bergen, but the walk along Bryggen is in fact more revealing of its medieval German past, when the Hanseatic traders dominated commerce along the Norwegian coast and Bergen was at the height of its power. The great fire of 1702 destroyed many Bryggen buildings but most were rebuilt and these Hanseatic houses are now on UNESCO's World Heritage list.

To keep your chronology correct, for the moment walk past these colourful buildings – just peeping sideways up the narrow wood-paved 'closes' that housed Bergen's early inhabitants – to **Bryggens Museum** (tel: 55-58-80-10), near the **Radisson SAS Royal Hotel**.

The Tracteursted

The museum had its birth in another of Bergen's catastrophic fires, in 1955, which led to the excavation of many archaeological treasures (some from the 12th century – sensitive reconstructions illustrate the life of that time). The Radisson SAS Royal Hotel also rose from the ashes of the 1955 fire when the architect, Oivind Maurseth, rebuilt six of the warehouse frontages, using original materials to do so.

Bryggen guides (often students) wear national costume for a tour that lasts around 1–1½ hours and includes Bryggen, the **Hanseatic Museum** (tel: 55-31-41-89), and **Schøtstuene** (Hanseatic Assembly Rooms; tel: 55-31-60-20). Parties are then led back through Bryggen's maze of lanes and wooden tenements, many of which have come to life again as shops, work-shops and restaurants. Here you will find **Bryggen Tracteursted** (tel: 55-31-40-46), a 300-year-old inn that claims to be the oldest in Nor-way. Bryggen is the place to try out Bergen's specialities, such as *skillingsboller*, saucer-sized biscuit-buns flavoured with cinnamon.

The Hanseatic Museum is housed in one of the oldest and best preserved merchant houses where merchants and apprentices once gathered in the big communal room, with its enormous beer jug and a dried Royal Cod (distinguished by a knob on its forehead) hanging above. So great was the fear of fire that not a single stove was allowed in these tall wooden houses even during the excruci-ating cold of a Bergen winter. The only relief for merchant and apprentice alike was Schøtstuene, the German assembly rooms in **Øvregaten**, Bergen's oldest street. In this centre of German social life, a fire was permitted, the beer flowed, and the apprentices had their school lessons.

You are now almost back at Bryggens Museum and nearby is **Mariakirken** (St Mary's Church), Bergen's oldest functioning build-ing. It dates from the 12th century, when the city was a centre of religious life with a cathedral and 20 churches. Mariakirken survived fires and war, has been altered and enlarged, and its finest trea-sure is the rich baroque pulpit, a German gift after Mariakirken became the Hanseatic League's church. The 15th-century Gothic triptych was probably made in Lübeck, and German was used for services until the 1920s.

Back at Vågen, **Fiskekrogen** specialises in fish and game and, given Norwegian restaurants are expensive, offers good value. Down by the harbour, sit outside for a beer (also not cheap) and then move into the small restaurant. The fish tank in the centre, watched over by a large stuffed bear, allows you to make your own choice. Fish soups are excellent (around 120NKR) and a main course varies

Inside the Mariakirken

from crayfish tails with saffron sauce to a *sautå* of salmon and shellfish which will cost between 200–300NKR.

After lunch head north again past the German wharfhouses. Take a quick look at the angular red brick building on the corner, which is Bergen's **Kjøttbasar** (meat market), built in 1876 but reopened in 1997 as a gourmet emporium, selling everything from fish cakes to caviar. Note the unicorn's head standing out from the first storey above the bar **Sjøboden**. Unicorn translates into the Norwegian **Enhjøringen**, the name of the seafood restaurant for tonight's evening meal (tel: 55-32-79-19; reservations recommended).

Past the Radisson SAS Royal Hotel, the first tall building is **Rosenkrantztårnet** in what was known first as Holmen, later Bergenhus, where the city had its beginnings. From the 12th century, this fortified area held the Royal Palace and military headquarters, and was also the centre of West Norway's religious life. In the 13th century, under King Håkon Håkonsson, Bergen became the capi-

Peace and tranquillity

tal of Norway and **Håkonshallen**, which you see next, was finished in 1261 for the coronation of Magnus Lagabøter (Lawmender). Rosenkrantztårnet – named after Erik Rosenkrantz, the Danish governor of Bergen during the 1560s – was built by stonemasons brought over from Scotland, which is why it looks very similar to a fortified Scottish house of the same period. The middle building between the tower and Håkonshallen is **Kommandant-boligen** (the Commandant's Residence) built in 1725 and now the official residence of Western Norway's military chief of staff; the interior is not open to the public.

In 1944, when Bergen was occupied by German troops, an explosion in Vågen caused terrible damage, but this provided the opportunity to restore the buildings of Bergenhus as closely as possible to their original forms. Now, Håkonshallen has a beautiful banqueting and concert hall and Rosenkrantztårnet's medieval floors have been re-created.

Though the walk back to the centre is short, you can pick up bus No 1 or 9 to the centre (**Torgalmenningen** or **Galleriet**), to rest and change at the hotel ready for the evening. **Enhjøringen**, which you passed earlier in Bryggen, was first mentioned in court evidence in 1304 by which time the German merchant, Herman Skult, had already lived there for 50 years; after the great fire of 1702, the house was rebuilt on its original foundations. Clamber up into the little series of rooms that form the restaurant, with its red beams, old furniture, and warm old-fashioned atmosphere.

Not surprisingly, Bergen is famous for its fish and there are several fine fish restaurants from which to choose. Try *gravet laks*, a salmon cured in a traditional way, and served with dill and a mustard-based sauce to start. Scandinavians are also reputed to be caviar enthusiasts, and a *kaviar trio*, three types of caviar with raw onion and fresh cream, is also good and tasty. In summer, a delicious seafood *smorgasbord* is offered by numerous Bergen restaurants. Another good recommendation is the **Kafe Krystall** (tel: 55-32-10-84), located on Kong Oscars Gate near to the fish market, behind the medieval Korskirken quarter, and detailed in *Practical Information (see page 75)*.

If you feel like searching out Bergen's authentic pub life at the end of the meal, go to **Sjøboden** for a final drink. It is usually full of sea-men and oil workers and can be very noisy on Friday and Saturday nights. There are many other options for an after-dinner drink *(see page 78)*.

10. Bergen Overview

From May 1–September 15 catch the Bergen Express sightseeing train for its circular tour of the city. Then head to the Domkirken (Cathedral). The White Lady harbour cruise fills the afternoon.

Begin the day at the Tourist Information Centre to book tickets for the **White Lady harbour cruise** at 2.30pm which leaves from the left-hand quay of the Fish Market (you can also book at the kiosk there), and enquire if the **Buekorps Museum** will be open on the

The Bergen Express

Bryggen in the sun

following day. Either here or in your hotel, enquire about **Fana Folklore** for the following evening (June to August only).

Walk south to **Torgallmenningen** and you are at the heart of Bergen's shopping centre, which extends left into **Strandgaten**. For later reference, take a quick look at the windows of **Sundt**, one of Bergen's biggest department stores, and the entrance to the shopping centre **Galleriet**, for lunch time. You can scarcely miss the national monument to seamen, a granite and bronze block which commemorates Norway's seafaring achievements from Viking times to the 20th century, with figures illustrating the Norsemen's 11th-century voyage to North America, the Norwegian voyages to Greenland, merchant ships and whaling, and finally Norway's 20th-century oil transport.

The **Bergen Express**, a little red-painted road train, takes off every hour from a stop in front of the Hanseatic Museum by the harbour, tel: 55-53-11-50. On its hour-long journey, the train heads along **Fjellveien**, the mountain road, and through one of the city's most distinctive old districts. From here it is easy to appreciate how much Bergen is a city of fjord, lake and mountain. The journey wends down past Mulen to Mariakirken, through Bergenhus and back along Bryggen and Torget to the starting point.

An alternative for this morning ride might be a shopping expedition, a light lunch or a waffle at a kiosk.

Back in the centre of the city, cross the wide road from Torget and take **Kong Oscars Gate** to **the Cathedral** (Domkirken) the only medieval church apart from Mariakirken to survive Bergen's ferocious fires. Though much of Bergen has had to be rebuilt, this

Picturesque street

On the waterfront

part of the city echoes the medieval city in its layout and style and the whole area of small criss-cross streets and squares lends itself to wandering. The area is delightful and is home to numerous antiques shops and cafés.

On the way to Domkirken, you see **Holy Cross Church** (Kors-kirken) to the right, but the church is rarely open. If you can get in, there are fragments of the earliest church (1150) but it was damaged by fire so many times, even before the great fire of 1702, that the cross-shaped building is now a mixture of styles.

Domkirken also faced war and fire but Magnus Lagabøter rebuilt it in the late 13th century and much of his nave and choir remain. After the Reformation it became Bergen's Reformed Cathedral, but was again a casualty during the 1665 Battle of Vågen, when an English cannonball ploughed into the wall above the west door. If you can time your visit for a Thursday, the organist gives a short recital at noon, which adds immensely to the true atmosphere of this sturdy cathedral. Next door is the **Cathedral School**, always known as the Latin School, where the Norwegian-born playwright and poet, Ludvig Holberg (commemorated in Grieg's *Holberg Suite*) had his education, before gravitating to Copenhagen at a time when Denmark still ruled Norway.

Galleriet on the south side of Torgallmenningen is one of three modern shopping centres, ideal when winter snows hit the city. The basement floor is like a huge garden of plants, the faint scent drifting up to the galleries above. Shops here aim to attract both locals and visitors. Melvaer, a first class bookshop with a great many books in English indicates Norwegian linguistic prowess, a sports shop has the latest in brand names and the good quality leather and knitwear is popular with visitors, as is gold and silver jewellery in the *gullsmed* (goldsmith) on the ground floor. **Kafe Augustus** (tel: 55-32-35-25) is on the top gallery.

Kafe Augustus is owned by the **Augustin Hotel** on the southern waterfront of Vågen and, as well as unusual soups, salads, hot and and cold dishes, has an excellent counter with cakes, pastries and

'Statsraad Lehmkuhl' lying at anchor

the ubiquitous *smørbrød* (open sandwich) big enough for a light meal at a cost of 60NKR upwards. A glass of wine will set you back a minimum of 50NKR but Kafe Augustus makes a pleasant place to sit and watch the passers-by.

Fjord excursions, which are highly recommended, can be taken from **White Lady pier** at the fish market. Three hundred thousand people arrive in Bergen each year by a variety of cruise ships. From a boat, it is easy to realise how much Bergen has depended upon the sea. The *White Lady's* one-hour harbour tour (1 May–31 August; four-hour cruises are also available from 1 May–30 September, for further information contact the Tourist Office or the pier at the fish market, tel: 55-25-90-00) leaves at 2.30pm and passes a continuous line of coloured wooden warehouses and fishing sheds, mostly still in use. The goal is a seaview of **Gamle Bergen** (Old Bergen) at **Elsesro**, an open-air museum where a group of 40 wooden houses from the 18th and 19th centuries are gathered.

Byfjorden

As the *White Lady* turns west across **Byfjorden**, Bergen's green islands begin to appear and at weekends the water is dotted with boats and sails. The island ahead is **Askøy**. The ferry turns next into **Puddefjorden**, slips under a high bridge and passes the quay used by the coastal steamer *(Hurtigruten)* that leaves around 10pm each night for its 3,579-km (2,224-mile) trip around Nordkap (North Cape) to Kirkenes on the Russian border and back. In summer

The Bellevue restaurant

Hurtigruten boats leave daily, and the journey between Bergen and Kirkenes takes 11 days, with stops at 35 ports. For further details, ask your travel agent. The steamers take cars and it's advisable to book well in advance. Passes are available for 16–25 year olds. Also contact Troms Fylkes Dampskibsselskap AS, tel: 77-64-82-00, fax: 77-64-81-80, email: booking@tfds.no or Ofotens og Vesteraalens Dampskibsselskab asa, Narvik, tel: 76-96-76-00 (information), 76-96-76-96 (bookings), fax: 76-96-76-01/11, email: booking@ovds.no, website: www.hurtigruten.com.

Heading for the **Nordnes Peninsula** you will catch a glimpse of **Frederiksberg Fortress** and, below it, the popular **Nordnes Sjøbad** (bathing place) which has an inviting heated outdoor pool where you can swim among the steam. At the tip of Nordnes Peninsula is the **Bergen Aquarium** (Akvariet).

Just down by the water is the excellent restaurant **Nordnes Ende**, which specialises in seafood. Located on the site of an old wharf, this place offers magnificent views over the water and Bryggen. Open for lunch and dinner, tel: 55-55-30-90.

11. Galleries and Museums

A day which includes visits to the National Theatre, Stenersen's Collection, Rasmus Meyer's Collection, Grieg Hall, Johannes Church, Natural History Museum and Maritime Museum. Lunch in the Lido Café. After lunch, via the Buekorps Museum to Nordnes Point, Aquarium and swimming pool. Evening: Fana Folklore (book through the hotel or Tourist Information Office).

Start off from **Ole Bulls Plass** beside the **Radisson SAS Hotel Norge**, Ole Bulls plass 4, tel: 55-57-30-00/30, fax: 55-57-30-01, just up the hill from Torgallmenningen. Ahead is the **National Theatre** (Den Nationale Scene), an art nouveau building which opened in 1909. Most productions are in Norwegian but, during the **Bergen International Festival** (music and drama) in the spring, you might find something in English. Ole Bull founded the theatre in 1850 (in a building destroyed during World War II) and the statue on the west side is of the nationalist and writer Bjørnstjerne Bjørnson, who was for a time director of the

The Grieg Hall

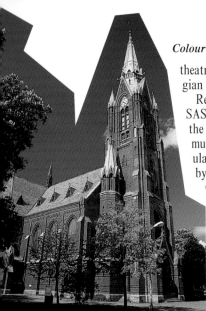

Colour contrast on Johannes Church

theatre and wrote the words for the Norwegian National Anthem.

Return to Ole Bulls Plass and Radisson SAS Hotel Norge and walk east towards the town park and Smålungeren, past the music pavilion where brass bands, very popular in Norway, play in the summer. Close by is a statue of the composer Edvard Grieg. Cross over **Christies Gate** and into the park. On the right of the lake three adjoining buildings hold the art collections but, if you plan to visit the museums, do not try to tackle them all in one morning.

The first two buildings house the **Bergen Art Museum** (tel: 55-56-80-00), which encompasses two different museums: **The Stenersen Collections** and **The Bergen Gallery** (Bergen Kunstforening). The Picassos and Klees of the Stenersen's Collection form a blazing contrast to Norway's most famous European painter, Edvard Munch, also well represented. The Fine Arts Society contains Norwegian paintings from the last 150 years; it is open throughout the year with changing exhibitions of contemporary art. **The Rasmus Meyer Collection**, in the next building, also features Norwegian artists such as J C Dahl, born in Bergen, and Harriet Backer, and holds works by Munch.

Leaving Meyer's collection, turn right to face **Grieg Hall** (Grieghallen), opened in 1978. Shaped like a grand piano, this unusual hall has contributed enormously to the success of the Bergen International Festival, and its acoustics are superb. It is the home of Norway's oldest orchestra, the Bergen Philharmonic, founded in 1765, which performs every Thursday and some Fridays from September to June. Follow **Lars Hilles Gate**, back across Christies Gate until you meet Torggaten. Turn left here and begin the long climb up cobbles and steps with the unmistakable red brick façade and green copper steeple of **Johanneskirken** ahead. This area, known as **Nygårdshøyden**, was built at the end of the 19th century to house the rich Bergensere. It is still the university area, with a cluster of museums, though many of the newer faculties have moved further out.

Take the diagonal path left across the grass beside the church for the **Natural History Museum**, a magnificent building from the end of

Tête-à-tête in the aquarium

the 19th century; known simply as 'The Museum', it is the kernel of the university. Once this area was called Hangman's Hill and it was the town's place of execution. Today, the peaceful gardens around the museum are the University Botanic Garden. At the far side, the **Historic Museum** covers art, culture, archaeology and ethnology. A tunnel at the foot of the museum's tower functions as a short cut into the **Møhlenpris** area.

To the right of the Historic Museum are two later buildings, the **University Library** and Bergen's Maritime Museum (**Sjøfarts-museum**; tel: 55-32-79-80), both opened in the early 1960s. The latter is probably the most evocative of this seafaring area and the exhibits range from Old Norse times to the present. Not far from the Historisk Museum on the other side is **Villaveien**, the street which preserves some of Bergen's magnificent 19th-century villas. After the stiff climb up, you may be thankful to walk back down for lunch. **Lido Café and Restaurant** (tel: 55-32-59-12) is at Torget, with a view of the fish market and a traditional buffet *smorbrød*.

After lunch, walk along Strandgaten from Torgallmenningen to a small, square building, similar to an old gatehouse, called **Muren**. The ground floor holds shops; the first floor was once a banqueting hall, now the **Buekorps Museum**. This private museum is rarely open (weekends only, closed in July), but in summer you can hardly miss the Buekorps, whose history goes back some 140 years. It is something like a boys' brigade; its members wear a distinctive uniform, and today still play their part in many local celebrations.

From here, Strandgaten becomes a pedestrian street. Turn left till you reach **Klostergaten** and walk along towards **Nordnes Point**. The area is a maze of old buildings and narrow lanes such as **Knøsesmauet**, which plunges steeply down between wooden buildings. The tower at the top was once a guardhouse, built in 1774. Further on, along Strangehagen and Galgebakken, is **Frederiksberg**, part of the 17th-century defensive walls.

Bergen's **Aquarium** (Akvariet; Nordnesbakken 4, tel: 55-55-71-71, May–September 9am–8pm, October–April 10am–6pm), which

The young generation of folk dancers

celebrated its 40th anniversary in 2000, has one of Europe's best collections of seals and penguins. Near here, try out another of Bergen's bathing places, **Nordnes Sjøbad**, with a heated outdoor pool. Afterwards, you can pick up the No 4 bus back, but the walk is only 15 minutes and, if you return via the Vågen side of the peninsula, you pass **Tollboden**, (Customs House) a beautiful building from 1744 which, though badly damaged by a 1944 explosion, has been restored. Further on is **Nykirken** (New Church), which belies its name – there has been a church here since the Middle Ages. It was last rebuilt in 1956 and its fine galleries can be seen to the rear. From here, it is not far to the Buekorps Museum, and thence, via Valkendorfsgaten and Trånplassen, which holds the **Bergen Court House** (Tinghuset), back to Torgallmenningen.

Tonight, you may choose to go to **Fana Folklore** (tel: 55-91-52-40, book ahead, June–August only) a traditional Norwegian evening designed as a country wedding. The main season is from June until the end of August but Fana Folklore is also open on some evenings in May and September. Buses leave **Festplassen** (across Christies Gate from the bandstand) at 7pm on Monday, Tuesday, Thursday and Friday for the half-hour journey to the old **Fanakirke** south-west of the city for a short recital of traditional tunes. You then go on to **Rambergstunet** (an old farm) to be greeted by a fanfare on the *lur*, an ancient musical instrument like a coaching horn. Guests sit at long wooden tables, with a view of the **Fana Fjord**, and enjoy traditional Norwegian cooking, music, dancing, and singing. An alternative to this colourful evening is the Tuesday and Thursday folklore programme given by the **Bergen Folklore Group** in Bryggens Museum (also June–August, tel: 55-31-95-50). Performances start at 9pm and, if you prefer to eat beforehand, many hotels have a tourist menu served up to 7pm.

12. Grieg's Troldhaugen

A morning or afternoon spent at Grieg's home at Troldhaugen and a a visit to Fantoft Stavkirke (Stave Church) on the way back to Bergen.

For the last 20 years of his life, Norway's most celebrated composer, Edvard Grieg, spent his summers at **Troldhaugen**, the elegant wooden house he built on a promontory above the peace of **Nordås Lake**, just off the E68 in the direction of **Fana** (southwest). Alongside the water is the writing *hytte* (hut) where he composed many of his best-known works. He was buried there and you can see his gravestone and that of his wife, the singer Nina Hagerup, down by the waterside where Grieg used to go fishing.

Inside Troldhaugen

Grieg was very much part of the flood of nationalism that swept through Norway during the 19th century. Born in Bergen in 1843, the composer was descended from a Scottish merchant, Alexander Greig, who emigrated from Aberdeen to Bergen in 1779. Grieg was greatly influenced by Norwegian folk music, and he and the violinist Ole Bull spent many weeks every year trekking through the great mountain massifs of Jotunheimen and Hardangervidda, transcribing traditional folk songs. Another product of these expeditions is his incidental music to Henrik Ibsen's *Peer Gynt*, based on stories from Vinstra, in Eastern Norway.

Troldhaugen is preserved exactly as Grieg left it, with his armchair, manuscripts, books, and his piano still in working order. In summer, recitals and concerts are held in the house, although most take place in **Troldsalen**, a hall in the grounds which holds 200 people.

Outside Troldhaugen

On the way back to Bergen, it's well worth making a visit to **Fantoft Stave Church**, located in the district of Paradis. Nothing is arguably more Norwegian than the *stavkirke* (stave churches), which get their name from their solid, upright timber trunks. With their roofs shaped like the curves of a Viking ship, these are churches belonging to a people hankering after their pagan past. The strength and structural integrity of such buildings render them capable of standing for hundreds of years, although many were destroyed during the 19th century and, sadly, only 28 remain in Norway today.

When it was decided by the village of Fortun to build a new church in 1883, Fantoft – instead of being demolished – was relocated to the Bergen area, thanks to the work of a far-sighted Bergenser, Konsul F Gade. Unfortunately, the church burnt down in June 1992, but it was recently rebuilt to its original 12th-century likeness.

Troldhaugen and Fantoft are easily accessed by car but are awkward to reach by bus and foot. The simplest way of getting there is on one of the Bergen guided tours that leave from, and return to, the Tourist Information Office (for details, *see Practical Information, page 90*).

The Fantoft Stave Church

13. Gamle Bergen

An afternoon by bus or car to Gamle Bergen, at Elsesro.

Bergen has long been renowned for the beauty of its wooden houses and, despite many fierce fires, a surprising number remain. **Gamle Bergen** (Old Bergen) is an attempt to show what Bergen must have been like in the 18th and 19th centuries by recreating a small West Norwegian community of some 40 houses brought in from various places to the old estate of Elsesro. To reach Gamle Bergen takes no more than 15 minutes on bus No 1 or 9 from the centre (behind the Post Office), Bryggen, or by car north-west on road 14.

The houses range across the social spectrum from the tiny **Sypikenshus** (the Seamstress's House), just a room and kitchen where she lived and plied her needle, to the grand ballroom of **Embetsmannshuset** (the Official's Residence) with French imperial-style wallpaper made in Paris in 1824 showing a Greek festival. **Barbersalongen** (the Barber's Shop), with heavy, padded seats and a comfortable masculine air was the place where the men met. It is full of 19th-century barbers' equipment, and **Kjøpmannshuset** (the Merchant's House) has much of the same comfort, particularly in the living room with its potted plants and stuffed sofas.

From a slightly earlier period, **Krohnstedet** is a wealthy country house, dated 1785, decorated for a party on 20 June 1808 and preserved in aspic at Gamle Bergen. When Louis Daguerre displayed his historic first photograph in Paris in 1839, the citizens of Bergen enthused and by 1852 the city had its own photographer. At Gamle Bergen, the **Photographer's Studio** dates from around 1900 and is full of fascinating contemporary equipment.

Statue of Edvard Grieg

However, most tempting of all is the aroma from **Bakerhuset** (the Baker's House), once situated just off Bryggen near Mariakirken. When the bakery is preparing the traditional pastries that are on sale in the Museum, the smells of the wood-fired stove and of the traditional recipes mingle temptingly.

The main estate building still stands in its original place and has a restaurant open from noon–7pm, May to September. The last tour is 4pm (in summer, earlier at other times) but if you are this late at Gamle Bergen, you might choose to eat early in the restaurant before the tour. Another alternative is to wander down towards the sea to swim at **Sandviken Sjøbad**, one of Bergen's best bathing places. Sea bathing in these sheltered waters, even this far north, is amazingly warm at the height of summer.

14. Fløyen

By funicular to Fløyen, Bergen's spectacular 'mountain'.

Make sure you have the Information Centre's leaflet and sketch map of **Fløyen**, *Gledes Kartet,* before you walk across to **Fløybanen's** bottom station on the far side of Torget and up past the Meat Market. Here the little funicular railway whisks up 320m (1,000ft) to the top station in something under eight minutes. Try to get into the lowest carriage for the most spectacular view of the Bergen panorama. On the return, sit here only if you have a head for heights though there is no need to be nervous. Fløybanen, Scandinavia's first cable railway, has been climbing smoothly up and down the mountain since 1918 without an accident.

From the top station, where there is a small coffee bar, restaurant and shop, Bergen below is a map of islands and peninsulas which lead gradually towards the North Sea. Seven protective hills shelter the city: Blåmanen, Rundemanen Sandviksfjellet and the distant Storsåta to the north, Damsgårdfjellet, Løvstakken to the west and Ulriken, to the south, at 642m (2,105ft) the highest of the seven, with its own cable car up to a top station and restaurant, and free concerts between June and August.

Fløyen, with its summer restaurant in a beautiful 1925 building nearby is Bergen's nearest open hill country, where people ski in winter and walk in summer. There are some 25km (15 miles) of track, all colour-coded to the sketch map. It is typical West Norwegian hill country, comprising woods, heath, peak and lake. One of the most pleasant and easiest walks is the track around **Skomakerdiket**, a popular bathing lake; for the more energetic, the track past **Brushytten** leads up to **Blåmanen**, some 552m (1,700ft) above a lake **Blåmansvannet**. None of the walks is more than 5km (3 miles). In summer, **Fløyen Restaurant** is a peaceful setting for a leisurely coffee or lunch on the verandah, and for shelter when it is wet.

It can be fun to walk down or, less energetic but nonetheless interesting, try taking the train to the **Fjellveien** station above the terminal, and stroll through **Fjellien** where the white wooden houses and cobbles have changed their character very little over many years. At the foot of the hill in Ovregaten is Bergen's oldest school, **Christi Krybbe** (Christ in the Crib), a primary school since 1740, and at No 17 you come to **GlasHuset**, which has been making and selling glass for over 40 years.

View of Bergen

15. Norway in a Nutshell

The steepest, narrowest, highest, fiercest, longest, most beautiful scenery in Norway. This tour sets off from Bergen, but it can also start from Oslo.

This West Norwegian itinerary gives you not only the scenery for which Norway has become justly famous but also a taste of the varied and comprehensive transport system. In summer, the tour starts by train from Bergen around 10am. It soon plunges into a tunnel, then bursts out again to reach the tranquil **Sørfjorden**, and winds its way along the fjord towards **Stanghella**.

The train then turns north-east through **Dale** and follows the water almost to **Voss**, centre of a rich farming district. After passing Voss (there is a short stop there on the way back) the train enters the longest tunnel on this part of the line, the 5km (3 mile) **Gravhals Tunnel**. At Myrdal, you change to a small train for **Flåm**,

Stone church in Voss

nearly 850m (2,800ft) below, down **Flåmsdalen** to the edge of **Aurlandsfjorden**, one of the innermost finger tips of **Sognefjord**, more than 156km (97 miles) from the sea. The Flåm line is a miracle of engineering, snaking 6km (4 miles) down the narrow mountain valley, through 20 tunnels and flickering in and out of winter snow screens. The gradient is the steepest in Europe used by a conventional train. **Kjosfossen** waterfall is at its most magnificent in May, and you get another chance to see the cascading waters between Kjosfossen and the Bakli tunnel.

This itinerary allows enough time for lunch at Flåm, which

is served at the **Fretheim Hotel** (tel: 57-63-22-00, fax: 57-63-23-03, not included in the ticket). Alternatively, try the Furukroa restaurant–café, a simple cafeteria offering good local specialities (tel: 57-63-23-25). After lunch, take the ferry along Aurlandsfjorden at the start of a two-hour voyage to Gudvangen. On both sides, mountains swoop into the water and every tiny water meadow has space for a farm or cluster of wooden houses. The biggest community along this fjord is **Aurland**, famous for its shoes. The ferry turns southwest into **Nærøyfjorden**, where the height of the mountains is double the width of the fjord. The next stop is **Gudvangen**, dwarfed by precipitous mountains, where you could overnight at the beautifully situated Gudvangen Fjordtell (tel: 57-63-39-29), and from here the tour continues by bus into **Nærøydalen**, past the entrance to the new tunnel from Gudvangen to **Landhuso** which will make it possible to make the whole journey by road. From the hairpin bends of the road up **Stalheimskleiven** (gorge) you can see two fine waterfalls, **Stalheimfossen** and **Sivlefossen**, named after the poet Per Sivle, whose childhood home stands above.

During World War II, the Stalheim Gorge was the scene of fierce fighting when Norwegian forces held out at the **Stalheim Hotel** (tel: 56-52-01-22), the highest point. Stalheim has been a coaching inn since the 17th century and the bus makes a welcome brief stop at the present hotel which is an excellent place to buy souvenirs. At Voss take the train to arrive back in Bergen at around 8pm.

Nature's tranquillity

16. Lysøen

A cultural and musical day on Ole Bull's island of Lysøen.

Lysøen, the last home of Norway's famed 19th-century violinist, Ole Bull, lies some 30km (19 miles) south-west of Bergen. This beautiful island in **Lysefjorden** has been inhabited since the Middle Ages, when it belonged to the monks of Lysekloster on the mainland. The ruins of their community can be visited if you have time.

Take the "Lysefjordruta" bus from platform 20 at Bergen bus station, and ask the driver to set you down at **Buena Quay** for the boat to Lysøen. By car, take road 1 out to **Nestun**, then follow signs to **Fana**, and the hill road over Fanafjell to the **Sørestraumen** crossroads. Turn right down to Buena Quay and Lysøen will be hard to miss. The Ole Bull ferry leaves for the island on the hour from noon–3pm, returning at 10 minutes to the hour up to 3.50pm (Sunday 11am–4.50pm). Sailings allow some three hours on the island, time enough to take the guided tour of the house and explore some of the paths which Bull constructed through natural woodland.

The house is an astonishing building with a strange onion dome tower. Bull called it his 'Little Alhambra'. He built it for his second wife, the American Sara Thorp, and the design was largely his own. It includes a recital room, seating 120. Inside, the house is Norwegian pine but every room is a mixture of styles, flamboyant carvings and decoration. One of Ole Bull's violins is on display here, but his greatest one is on show in West Norway's Museum of Applied Arts in Bergen. The music room is a rich cavern showing the influences of Bull's travels. There is also a highly unsuccessful piano designed by Bull, which he turned into a solid desk.

The house is full of gifts from admirers: a tapestry in the bedroom made by ladies of the Russian court, an 80-stone diamond ring from the Czar. When Ole Bull died in 1880, 14 ships escorted his coffin to Bergen and 25–30,000 people attended his funeral. His wife and daughter continued to spend summers on Lysøen, as did his granddaughter, Sylvea Bull Curtis, who preserved the building and island until 1973, when she donated the estate to the Norwegian Society for the Preservation of Historical Monuments; they re-opened it as a museum in 1984. A bust of Sylvea Bull Curtis by Hans Jacob Meyer stands in the garden in front of the house.

Throughout the summer, and particularly during the **Bergen International Festival** (held in May and June, for information tel: 55-21-06-30 or visit: www.fib.no), the old music room resounds to Bull's music, with violin recitals and small ensembles. Advance booking is necessary (tel: 55-31-21-70), and the audience travels out from Bergen by special coach.

Musical climax at the Bergen festival

Shopping

What to Buy

The first thing to remember is that Norwegian goods are high quality and often highly priced. That does not mean that they are not good value, particularly if you take advantage of the tax-free schemes with savings of 10–15 per cent. Norway is the only Scandinavian country in which visitors from the British Isles can claim VAT refunds. Pick up a brochure at the tourist office, or tel: 67-14-99-01, fax: 67-14-97-84 for details. In the shop, you pay in full and collect a 'cheque' for the amount. The tax portion is refunded on the way out of the country from special tax-free representatives (not customs officers) at airports, ports, and frontiers.

Almost all Norway's museums and galleries have a shop which sells a variety of interesting and typical items. The most frequent souvenir is a **troll**, of every shape and degree of ugliness. Up in the mountains, surrounded by the weird outlines of rocks and trees, it is easy to understand how Norwegians came to believe in the mythology of the troll, unfriendly creatures which lived in the mountains and came out at night to do their mischief.

Looking for something typical, I much prefer a piece of *rosemaling* (**rosepainting**) – delicately painted wooden plates and household items, in patterns particular to different areas.

Most children love **dolls** in the traditional *bunader* or national costumes, which also vary tremendously from

A troll keeps an eye on shoppers

region to region. Sami (Lapp) craftwork includes similar dolls in their distinctive costume. Authentic work is labelled *Sami Duodji*.

Traditional skills have often been adapted to modern designs. The decorated *bunad* includes beautiful metal **jewellery**, so it is no surprise that gold and silverwork is excellent in Norway. Norway also has a lot of minerals, precious and semi-precious **gemstones**, often used in designs, including a beautiful slightly-mottled pink stone that is a bit like the traditional Greenlandic *tutapit*. Enamelled silver jewellery is very striking. In the same way, the tradition of **wood carving** continues in the production of an attractive range of bowls and other utensils.

Norwegian **knitted jackets**, sweaters and socks are famous. Again, the patterns vary according to the region and knitters in Setersdal and Fana are reputed to be among the best. Like the *bunad*, Norwegian **sweaters** are durable enough to hand down to the next generation and the silver clasps are very beautiful. Occasionally new patterns appear and the one designed for Norway's Winter Olympic team by the Dale Knitwear Company is very popular, and even the locals wear them.

Glass and porcelain are good buys, the former traditionally having a slightly grey tint, which is still seen in some modern glass. All three main glassworks at Hadeland, Magnor, and Randsfjorden welcome visitors to watch glass-blowing, and have retail shops.

Anyone who has visited the north of Norway knows that a **fur coat** is a way of keeping alive in winter. Norwegians excel at making goods like this, which fit in with the way of life and climate. It is the same with **sport and outdoor equipment**, such as boots (not cheap) that really keep out the cold and wet. And nowhere will you find a better or more comfortable rucksack. One I purchased at a sale in Oslo, designed for schoolchildren's day-to-day use, is big enough for overnight necessities. If it is **food** you are after, you could take home a packet of the cured salmon, *gravet laks*, which gives a true flavour of Norway. On the alcoholic front, *Akvavit* (a type of

schnapps) is the traditional Norwegian firewater.

Hours

Shopping hours are usually 9am–4.30/5pm, though you will find variations, with late night on Thursday (sometimes also Friday) usually to 7pm, Saturday 9am–2pm. Many new shopping malls in Bergen and Oslo stay open longer, sometimes until 8pm on weekdays, 6pm on Saturday. Grocery stores tend to open 9am–9pm during the week and 9am–6pm on Saturday.

Eating

What to Eat

As in other northern peasant societies, Norway's traditional cooking was, and in some senses still is, based on food that could be grown and raised in a short summer or taken from the sea, even in winter, and preserved for harder times. Dried, salted and smoked meats *(spekemat)* were always staple foods, along with dried, cured

and pickled fish, particularly herring. Kept in a barrel in the corner of the kitchen for months on end, this was part of the regular diet. Butter- and cheese-making left milk residues that could also be turned into various foods. Today, although this humble fare has evolved into something more refined, dried, cured and marinated fish and meat still remain important ingredients in Norwegian cooking. Hotels usually offer a selection of specially prepared fish and cooked meat on the breakfast table as well as later in the day. This breakfast table will usually be graced with a particularly fruity jam, not as stiff and oversweet as some and also surprisingly good with cereals.

Fish, from cod and mackerel to trout and salmon, is excellent, and *fiskeboller* (fish balls in a béchamel sauce) are regulars on every family's menu, served along with the plain, boiled potatoes that appear with even greater regularity. A sprinkling of fresh dill and butter lifts them out of the everyday. A big speciality is salmon,

fresh baked or boiled, smoked with a flavour that is particular to its area, or served as *gravet laks* – uncooked but cured salmon, served very thinly sliced with a dill or mustard-based sauce and sprigs of dill. Shellfish is also popular; crabs, lobster and prawns are favourites for *smørbrød*.

Even today, Norwegian specialities are often prepared from ingredients preserved in traditional ways. In many places, particularly on the west coast, *klippfisk* (split dried cod) is used in a variety of recipes and it is sometimes adapted to the cuisines of other countries, for example a *klippfisk* version of *bacalao* is popular on certain parts of the west coast. A delicacy for the Norwegian palate, though foreigners rarely appreciate the chewy texture, is *lutefisk*. This is fish marinaded in *lye* (dictionary definition: 'a strong alkaline solution; a liquid used for washing') and an acquired taste. The *akvavit* (a grain- or potato-based spirit; often flavoured with caraway) or *øl* (beer) that is traditionally served with *lutefisk* helps novices to wash it down, but for many people, the dish is viewed more as a challenge than a meal.

Fine ingredients for sale

The *koldtbord*, the cold table, which is popular throughout Scandinavia, although each country has its own distinctive style, is far more than its name suggests. On high days and holidays – and often at lunchtime in hotels – it starts with varieties of herring, goes on through fish, shellfish, fish cakes, patés and cold meats and, despite the name, continues with hot dishes, followed by cheese and puddings. The correct way of eating is not to pile your plate but to return to the table, taking small quantities each time. This is not a meal to be eaten in a hurry. *Akvavit*, perhaps chased with beer, is also a good accompaniment to pickled herrings that start *Det store koldtbord*.

Norway has an abundance of berries and mushrooms in forest and hillside from late spring into autumn, and these are available in markets in season. Berry-picking is popular enough over a week-end to make Monday-morning stained fingers almost fashionable. Best of all to my taste is *multer,* a yellow-coloured berry that is akin to a cloud berry, but there are also *blåbær* (blueberries or blakeberries) and wild strawberries, which have a peculiarly delicate taste. Try them all with sour cream.

The range of breads and pastries available is wide. *Flatbrød* is good with cheese, and dark-coloured rye bread makes the best base for the many stronger-tasting sandwich ingredients.

Eating out in Norway has never been cheap but since the 1980s the range and style of restaurants has expanded enormously, and in Oslo, Stavanger and Bergen, particularly, an influx of foreign restaurants has added to the choice – it is wise to remember, however, that these are not of the cheap take-away variety travellers will come across in many parts of the world. Even so, the prices can sometimes be competitive and if your funds are short you can always try *pølser*, a kind of hot dog, or *vaffler* (waffles) from a street kiosk. Even better, walk into a fishmongers and buy a fish cake or smoked salmon sandwich.

Recommendations

The following list includes restaurants already suggested under individual itineraries. A rough price guide for dinner per head without wine is as follows:
$$$:   400–600-plus NKR
$$:   200–300NKR
$:   under 200NKR
A quick and simple meal at lunchtime should cost well below 150NKR.

Oslo

BAGATELLE
Bygdøy Allé 3
Tel: 22-12-14-40
This culinary institution under the leadership of master chef Eyvind Hellstrom has two Michelin stars and a very relaxed ambience. You can choose from a five-, six- or seven-course meal. *$$$*

BØLGEN & MOI BRISKEBY
Løvenskiolds gate 26
Tel: 24-11-53-53
Trond Moi, Norway's highest-profile chef, has been expanding his empire with his wine-expert partner Toralf Bolgen, and what began at the Henie/Onstad Museum outside of Oslo is now spreading across Norway. In this former power station – innovatively renovated and redesigned in chic, postmodern style in Autumn 2000 – there is a *haute cuisine* dining room on the upper level, while more casual dining is offered downstairs. Have a drink at the bar and test the culinary waters. *$$$*

BRASSERIE HANSKEN
Akersgaten 2
Tel: 22-42-60-88
Near Aker Brygge, this popular restaurant attracts local movers and shakers, who come here for seafood and meat specialities. Sophisticated yet warm ambience. *$$/$$$*

EAST SUSHI ZONE
Frognerveien 10
Tel: 22-44-46-26
and:
Aker Brygge Bryggetorget 7
Tel: 22-83-63-51
This fast-growing chain of exotic noodle and sushi cafes can be found throughout Oslo. Quick, healthy and delicious food. *$/$$*

ENGEBRET CAFÉ
Bankplassen 1
Tel: 22-33-66-94
Serves a generous lunchtime *koldtbord* and an *à la carte* menu at night. See *Oslo Itinerary 2*. *$$*

FEINSCHMECKER
Balchens Gate 5
Tel: 22-44-17-77
This slightly formal but friendly restaurant offers a daily menu according to season as well as an *à la carte* selection with the focus on seafood. The dessert menu is worth considering, as the ice creams and sorbets are homemade. The selection of cheeses is also very good. *$$$*

FRU HAGEN
Thorvald Meyers Gate 40
Tel: 22-35-67-87
The popular Fru Hagen, in the heart of the trendy 'working class' quarter, Grünnenløkka, incorporates a cafe and restaurant next door to each other. The young, hip crowd come for the chicken and sweet chilli ciabattas, salads, or Thai wok specialities. *$/$$*

GAMLE RAADHUSET RESTAURANT
Nedre Slottsgate 1
Tel: 22-42-01-07
Traditional food, particularly seafood, in one of Oslo's oldest buildings. See *Oslo Itinerary 2*. *$$*

GRAND CAFÉ (GRAND HOTEL)
Karl Johans Gate 31
Tel: 22-42-93-90
See *Oslo Itinerary 3*. *$$*

KOKOPELLI
Ingelbrecht Knudssonsgate 1
Tel: 22-60-33-04
This modern restaurant in the heart of Oslo's antiques quarter serves up sandwiches, salads and omelettes for

lunch in its cellar dining room and *à la carte* dinner items on its upper level. Service is friendly and the ambience is comfortable. You can also drop in for an afternoon *latte*. $/$$

LANTERNEN KRO
Kro Huk Aveny 2, Bygdøy
Tel: 22-43-78-38
Lanternen Kro is a traditional inn and steakhouse in an old Oslo setting. *See Oslo Itinerary 3.* $$

MARES BRASSERIE
Frognerveien 12B
Tel: 22-54-89-80
Opened in 1999, this chic yet relaxed brasserie in the stylish Frogner quarter offers fresh seasonal fish and shellfish, with an excellent wine list presided by its Venetian-born proprietor. The lobster soup and oysters in season are a great way to start the evening. $$

NAJADEN RESTAURANT
Bygdøynesvn 37
Tel: 22-43-81-80
Part of the Maritime Museum on Bygdøy. *See Oslo Itinerary 3.* $$

PUNJAB SWEET HOUSE
Grønland 24
Tel: 22-17-20-86
If you fancy something spicy and you also want to check out Oslo's latest developing neighbourhood,

this is the place. Dishes include lamb curry, keema nan, kebabs, chicken tikka. Classic Indian cooking in an unpretentious atmosphere. $

RAYMOND'S MAT OG VINHUS
Ruseløkkveien 59
Tel: 22-83-69-90
This small, intimate restaurant serves fresh fish and lamb in a variety of ways, with some Mediterranean influence. Must be booked in advance. $$/$$$

RESTAURANT MAGMA
Bygdøy Allé 53
Tel: 23-08-58-10
Sonja Lee and her husband Laurent Sur-Nille worked in Provence with Alain Ducasse before launching Damien Hirst's 'Pharmacy' restaurant in London. In April 2000, they relocated to Oslo to offer unpretentious rustic cuisine to a stylish crowd. Modern art complements the decor. $$$

SOLSIDEN OYSTER BAR/RESTAURANT
Akershus Kai 34
Tel: 22-33-36-30
This place, which serves fresh fish and fine wines, is in a prime location on

At your service

the harbour. Open spring and summer. From October to March enjoy seafood specialities at their 'winter' restaurant, Havet, Pilestredet 31, tel: 22-20-34-45. *$$*

STORTORVETS CAFE AND RESTAURANT
Gjæstgiveri Grensen 1
Tel: 22-42-88-63
Stortorvets is basically a traditional old inn. However, it's a jazz café at lunch time and there's also jazz on Fridays. *$$*

SULT
Thorvald Meyers Gate 26
Tel: 22-87-04-67
If you can't stand noise or waiting for a table, go somewhere else in this hip, young neighbourhood. Otherwise, be patient, take a seat at the small bar and join the party. Fresh seafood is the speciality, cooked any way you like and served with various potato dishes that make ideal accompaniments. Nice wines by the glass plus the local fire water. *$$*

THEATERCAFÉEN (HOTEL CONTINENTAL)
Stortingsgate 24
Tel: 22-82-40-50
Haunt of artists and the intelligentsia. *See Oslo itinerary 3. $$*

VEGETA VERTSHUS
Munkedamsvn 3
Tel: 22-83-40-20
A popular vegetarian restaurant with a self-serve buffet. *$*

WOLLANS
Rådhusgata 28
Tel: 22-41-19-14
People smiled when this seafood restaurant opened on the site of a former sex shop (previously a fishmonger's). These days the decor is light, the ambience is relaxed and the clientele is keen to sample the

seasonal selection of fish and shellfish cooked with regional ingredients. *$$*

Bergen

BALTAZAR CAFE
Kjottbasaren, Vetridsallm 2
Tel: 55-55-22-10
(same location as Von der Lippe)
Casual dining from around the world. Salads, sandwiches and traditional Norwegian dishes. Open daily for lunch and dinner. *$$*

BRYGGESTUEN & BRYGGELOFTET
Bryggen 11
Tel: 55-31-06-30
Two restaurants in one of the old Hanseatic wharfhouses with a good atmosphere. Whale meat, reindeer and other Norwegian specialities when in season. A mecca for most visitors. *$$*

ENHJØRNINGEN
Bryggen
Tel: 55-32-79-19
A wharfhouse restaurant serving fresh seafood. *$$/$$$*

FINCKEN
Nygårdsgaten 2A
This ultra-hip cafe has a cool, minimal interior, good music and a primarily gay clientele. Open late. *$*

FISKEKROGEN
Zachariasbryggen
Tel: 55-31-75-66/55-55-96-60
Excellent seafood served in an intimate setting. *$$*

KAFE KRYSTALL
Kong Oscars Gate 16
Tel: 55-32-10-84
This 'secret' address is just minutes from the fish market behind the medieval Korskirken Quarter. With only six tables and a delightful 1920s' decor, eating here feels like

dining in the house of an elegant aunt. The menus changes daily offering a chance to have a menu of varied courses, featuring fish, shellfish, game and vegetables. Excellent wine list. *$$*

LUCULLUS
Valkendorfsgate 8
Tel: 55-30-68-00
Young chef Frederik Hald has made this restaurant within the Neptun Hotel the address for fine dining. Attentive service, elegant ambience and innovative menus that change seasonally and focus on regional ingredients. *$$$*

MUNKESTUEN
Klostergaten 12
Tel: 55-90-21-49
A tiny restaurant operated by a dedicated husband-and-wife team focussing on French cuisine and fine wines. Reserve. *$$/$$$*

NORDNES ENDE MARITIME RESTAURANT
Nordnes Ende peninsula
Tel: 55-55-30-90
This excellent fish restaurant in a converted wharfside shed is in a great location on the waterfront. Unusual snacks are served in the afternoons, as well as a lunch menu. For dinner there's a seasonal *à la carte* menu. *$$*

OLE BULL RESTAURANT
(RADISSON SAS HOTEL NORGE)
Ole Bulls Plass
Tel: 55-57-30-00
A superb *koldtbord* is served from noon–6pm, and there are also light meals and an *à la carte* menu. *$$*

SMAUET MAT & VINHUIS
Vaskerelvsmauet 1
Tel: 55-21-07-10
This popular spot attracts locals who come for fresh fish and game when is season. Nice wines by the glass. The open kitchen provides a bit of action amidst the cosy, noisy ambience. *$$*

SOPHIES CAFE
Vetrlidsallmenning 15
Tel: 55-96-20-10
This popular lunch spot attracts local workers in the week but it's also busy at weekends. Simple, delicious food at reasonable prices in a cosy ambience. There are two separate restaurants, a tapas bar and an Indian curry house in the same complex. *$*

VÅGEN FETEVARE
Kong Oscarsgate 10
This cosy cafe, which opens at 8am in the week, attracts a young and hip crowd. The coffees and basic open-faced sandwiches on fresh baked bread are very good, but don't leave without trying the chocolate cake. *$*

ZUPPERIA
Nordahl Bruns gate 9
Tel: 55-55-81-14
This popular 'soup kitchen' – even dessert soups are available – within the West Norway Museum of Decorative Art has its own entrance and its own opening hours. Fast, delicious food daily from 11am until midnight. Sandwiches and salads also available. *$*

Nightlife

In summer, the light lingers so long in Norway that it almost seems a crime to go inside. Night-time entertainment arrived here late, though, principally because of the ferocity of former anti-drinking laws, the residue of a strict Lutheran piety that led to prohibition in World War I. Outlawing of alcohol continued into the 1920s and only a change of government brought about its repeal. Thereafter, the state has had a monopoly on all imports of wines and spirits, and also runs Vinmonopolet (alcohol shops) where you buy alcohol at a high price.

Drink laws were only loosened in the 1980s, and although there was no reduction in prices, oil-rich Norwegians, at least in the cities, plunged into a style of life that extended into the small hours. Interestingly, however, the concept of 'buying a round' is not as typical in Norway as elsewhere, mainly because alcoholic drinks are there so expensive.

With the relaxation of drinking restrictions, hotels have gradually begun to add nightclubs, and the club age, particularly in Oslo, has brought a sudden rush of clubs/pubs/cafés that stay open until the early hours. Note, however, that these late-night establishments are not nightclubs in the sense that people will be dressy and the surroundings luxurious. They are more typically in the style of pubs where you can dance and drink late.

One important point: in Norway the drink-driving laws are very fierce and it's prudent not to drink any alcohol at all when in charge of a car. A familiar sight on a Saturday and Sunday morning is a Norwegian walking back to pick up his vehicle from where it was left the night before.

The Grieghallen

For concert lovers, Oslo and Bergen both have symphony orchestras, and their concert halls play host to many artistes outside the classical world. On the theatre front, Oslo has a National Theatre, although most plays are performed in Norwegian. The cinema is usually accessible here, since Scandinavians rarely dub English-language material, using sub-titles instead.

Oslo

Check in *What's On In Oslo* for details on clubs, as they open and close

with rapidity. The following lists a few established venues. Most big hotels also have a club or late-night bar.

CHAGALL (VICTORIA THEATRE)
Karl Johans Gate 35
Tel: 22-42-75-26
Open until 2am Friday, 4am Saturday. Disco every night. Over 20s only.

ROCKEFELLER MUSIC HALL
Torggata 16
Tel: 22-20-32-32

Wonderful setting in the old Torgata baths. Occasional concerts with some big names are held here. Over 20s only on normal nights; over 18s only for concerts.

SMUGET
Rosenkrantzgate 22
Tel: 22-42-52-62
Live jazz, blues and rock until 4am nightly. *A la carte* meals until 3.15am

Bergen

The Radisson SAS Hotel Norge, (NITE SPOT), Rosenkrantz (RUBINEN) and Radisson SAS Royal (ENGELEN) all have clubs, which stay open until 3am.

BANCO ROTTO
Vågsallmenningen
Tel: 32-75-20
Music and dancing in an elegant setting 10pm–2.30am Friday and Saturday.

DYVEKES VINKJELLER
Hollendergaten 7
Tel: 55-32-30-60
Bergen's oldest wine bar, with a popular terrace in summer and medieval ambience in the cellar. Excellent wines are sold by the glass.

MAXIME
Ole Bulls Plass
Tel: 55-30-71-20
Popular disco, food and drink spot Wednesday to Sunday until 3am.

RICK'S CAFE AND SALON
Veiten 3
Tel: 55-55-31-31
Eating, drinking, music and dancing

THE SCOTSMAN
Valkendorfsgate 1B
Tel: 55-55-87-75
Lively spot serving pub food upstairs. Live music Monday to Saturday.

Calendar of Special Events

The Norwegian passion for the outdoors means that many of the best annual events are sports based: skiing and ski-jumping in winter, and fishing and other outdoor festivals in summer. Street races and cycle marathons are also popular. At the end of June, Oslo turns out to welcome the competitors in **Den Store Styrkeprøven** cycle marathon from Trondheim. In May, Bergen has its **7 Fjellsturen**, an enthusiastic mountain walk over the city's seven hills. In March there is Oslo's ski festival, the **Holmenkollen Festival,** which attracts thousands out to the great ski jump in the Nordmarka. In the summer, the city's Bislett Stadium is the venue for an international athletics meeting, the **Mobil Bislett Games**.

Norwegians celebrate their **Constitution Day** on 17 May with enormous zeal but, thankfully, no displays of military might: just children who appear as a kaleidoscope of red, white and blue under the waving flags.

The biggest celebrations are in Oslo, concentrated around Karl Johans Gate, leading up to the Royal Palace. But each community will have its own distinctive festivities and, in Bergen, a lively and important part of the parade is the Buekorps, an association similar to the Boys' Brigade *(see page 57)*.

Midtsommer on 23 June is often a family party though there are also public celebrations. Their dark northern winters lead Scandinavians almost to worship the light. The centrepiece today is still the bonfire, around which people eat, drink, dance, sing, play games and stay up late on what is the lightest night of the year.

Bergen can claim the biggest arts festival in Norway, the **Bergen International Festival** in May and June (for information, tel: 55-21-06-30, fax: 55-21-06-40 or visit: www.fib.no). The festival, which started in the early 1950s, emphasises classical and other music but there is also theatre and ballet. The focal point is the Grieghallen,

Carnival in Bergen

named after Norway's most famous composer, but there are other venues. A **Night Jazz Festival**, a **Children's Festival**, and folk music and dancing take place at the same time. Oslo has a **Jazz Festival** in August.

Norwegian national holidays are as follows: Easter; Labour Day (1 May); Constitution Day (17 May); Ascension Day; Whitsun; Christmas and Boxing Day and New Year's Day. The lists below give the main events in each city.

OSLO

January–February
Lillehammer Ski Festival (January). Entertainment and contests in Lillehammer, in the mountains 1½ hours north of Oslo.

March
Holmenkollen Ski Festival.

May–June
Summer Kollen (June). Concerts, classical, pop, jazz and other entertainment around Holmenkollen Ski Jump. **Midtsommer** (23 June). Midsummer festival.
Den Store Styrkeprøven (end June). Cycle marathon all the way from Trondheim to Oslo.

July–August
Mobil Bislett Games (July), international athletics at Bislett Stadium.
Jazz Festival and concerts.
The Norway Cup, international youth soccer, with 1,000 teams of boys and

girls, which takes place in Ekeberg.
Maridalspelet (mid-August). Open-air historical drama, taking place in church ruins at Maridalen.

September–October
National Autumn Exhibition (September). New graphic art, painting, sculpture, Kunstnershus.
Oslo Marathon (September).
Contemporary Music Festival (October).

November–December
Nobel Peace Prize awarded in the University Aula (December).

BERGEN

May–June
Bergen International Festival and **Night Jazz Festival** and **Exhibition**. **Midtsommer** (23 June). Midsummer.

May–August
Art Exhibition. Exhibition and demonstration of old Norwegian culture and crafts, held in Rosendal.

July–September
Fishing Festival (early July) in the city centre.
North Sea Festival (mid-July). Historical festival.
Grieg Concerts at Troldhaugen, the composer's home.
Concerts also take place at Ole Bull's home at Lysøen.
Rosendal Barony Concerts at Bergen (July).
Baronispelet, drama at Rosendal.
Norwegian Film Festival (August).

Practical Information

GETTING THERE

By Air

Scandinavian Air Systems (tel: 0845 607 2772, fax: 020 8990 7127, www. sas.se) offer daily flights from London Heathrow and flights daily except Saturday from Manchester to Oslo International Airport, Gardermoen. **Braathens** (tel: 0191 214 0991, www. braathens.no), the main carrier within Norway, flies daily from London Stansted and six days per week from Newcastle to Oslo and Bergen.

British Airways (tel: 0345 222111; www. british-airways.com) run around five flights daily from London (Gatwick and Heathrow) to Oslo. **Air UK** (tel: 0990 074 074) fly from London Stansted, Aberdeen, Humberside and Teeside to Bergen.

Oslo International Airport and Bergen's Flesland Airport are both connected by bus services to the centre of town. Oslo also has a fast train shuttle, which takes under 20 minutes to reach the city centre from the airport.

Ryanair operate bargain flights twice daily from London Stansted to Oslo Torp airport at Sandefjord, 130km (80 miles) south of the capital. Buses transport visitors into Oslo. For details tel: 0870 333 1250 or 0541 569 569 or visit www.ryanair.com.

By Rail

International trains arrive at Oslo Central (Oslo-S) from all over Europe and Norwegian State Railways (NSB) provides a comprehensive and efficient internal network. Even the worst winter weather rarely stops the Oslo-Bergen line.

The NSB head office is at Jernbanetorget 2 (tel: 22-36-37-80). In Bergen, the station is on Strømgaten (tel: 55-96-69-00 or 55-96-69-61).

By Sea

Oslo car ferries run to and from Copenhagen, Kiel, Hirtshals (Denmark) and Fredrikshavn (Denmark).

Bergen car ferries arrive from and depart to Newcastle (Britain), the Faroe Islands and Iceland.

By Road

Formalities on the majority of border entry points are efficient and, once you are in Scandinavia, almost non-existent. Both Bergen and Oslo levy a modest charge for bringing a car into the city centre, which is collected at toll booths.

Do *not* drink and drive. Penalties are stiff (up to 10,000NKR, and in some cases even imprisonment) and the limit very low (0.5ml). A half-litre of beer could be too much. Norwegian medicines to be avoided before driving are marked with a red triangle.

TRAVEL ESSENTIALS

Passports and Visas

For the citizens of most countries, a valid passport is all that is required.

Customs, Excise and Duty Free

Visitors aged over 20 years can bring in one litre of spirits and one litre of wine, or two litres of wine, plus two litres of beer. Europeans over 16 years can bring in 200 cigarettes or 250g tobacco. Visitors over 16 from non-European countries may bring 400 cigarettes or 500g tobacco. One kilo of chocolate and sweets and other goods up to 1,000NKR are allowed (items for personal use are usually excluded).

Time Zone

Scandinavian time is GMT +1, and from March to September GMT +2.

Main Post Offices

Oslo: Dronningensgt 15 (entrance at Tollbugt). **Bergen**: Småstrandgt 3.

Telephones

To call other countries, first dial the international access code 095, then the relevant country code: Australia (61); France (33); Germany (49); Italy (39); Japan (81); Netherlands (31); Spain (34); United Kingdom (44); US and Canada (1). If you are using a US credit phone card, dial the company's access number, followed by the country code etc. AT&T, Tel: 8001-9011.

Directory enquiries: For numbers in Norway and Scandinavia, dial 0180; other countries 0181; telegrams, 0138.

Norway's international code is 47. The city code for Oslo is 22 and Bergen is 55 (the 0 is dropped when phoning from outside Norway). City codes are not used within their own areas.

Climate

In Oslo, winter day temperatures average -2°C (28°F) and 5° less at night. Bergen is slightly warmer but wetter and snow rarely lies heavily for long. Average summer temperatures for the whole country are around 16°C (60°F) and in Oslo around 22°C (71°F).

What to Wear

Norwegians tend to dress informally and stylishly in Oslo and Bergen. In summer, you should be warm enough if you wear light clothes, but it's wise to take sturdy shoes/boots, an anorak or raincoat and an umbrella with you as well, as it does rain a lot. The winter calls for very warm clothes. Norwegian hotels and houses tend to be warm, so its best to dress in layers. Mitts, gloves and hats, plus sunglasses or goggles are essential.

MONEY MATTERS

The currency is the Norwegian krone (NKR) divided into 100 øre. Notes are in 50, 100, 500 and 1,000 denominations; coins in 1, 5, 10.

You can bring unlimited amounts of currency into Norway but you may not take out more than 5,000NKR (plus the money you brought in).

Banks, post offices, airports, large tourist hotels, foreign exchange bureaux in Oslo and Tourist Offices in Oslo and Bergen, change foreign currency, travellers' cheques and Eurocheques; most banks will issue cash against credit cards. You can pay in most shops with Visa, Mastercard or Cirrus/Maestro and these cards may also be used to draw money out of cash machines.

Banking hours are Monday to Friday 8.30am–3.30pm (Thursday until 5pm).

GETTING AROUND

Oslo

Public Transport: Oslo has an excellent public transport service. There are eight underground lines (SST), converging at Stortinget, and five tram routes. Bus routes all converge on Jernbanetorget. Ferries connect the Oslofjord islands to the mainland from Vippertangen (bus 29 from Jernbane torget) and the Bygdøy ferry leave from Pier 3 outside the Rådhuset. Fo transport queries, tel: 177, Monda to Friday 7am–8pm, Saturday, Sun day, holidays 8am–6pm).

Taxis: Call Oslo Taxicentral on 81 54-48-15 or 22-38-80-90.

Cars: It is imprudent to use a ca in central Oslo, but for journeys out side it can be helpful. Good motor ing maps for the Greater Oslo are available from the Tourist Informa tion Centre. **Car-hire firms** are a follows: Avis, Billingstadsletta 14 (tel 81-53-30-44); Hertz, tel: 67-16-80 00; Budget, Sonja Heniesplass 4, tel 22-17-10-50. Oslo sightseeing taxi, tel 22-38-80-90. **Breakdown Service** operating 24-hour services include Falken (tel: 22-95-00-00); NAF Auto mobile Association (tel: 22-34-14-00) or Viking (tel: 22-08-60-00).

Bergen

Public Transport: Bergen has a goo network bus and ferry network. Fo times, consult HSD *Rutehefte,* a fre schedule available from the HSD Trans port Company, C. Sundtsgate 36 (te 55-23-87-00) and on local ferries an at bus stations. The Central Bus Sta tion at Strømgaten (tel: 55-55-90-9C or for general information, 177) is th terminal for all services to the Berge environs and the airport bus. There no special visitor bus ticket but you ca buy a 48-hour unlimited bus trave ticket, available on the buses.

Bergen has no internal **train** servic (only the summer sightseeing Berge Express, designed to show visitors th most famous sights in a one-hour tour Main-line trains from Oslo and statior en route arrive and depart at Strøn gaten Station (tel: 55-96-69-00). The are funicular railways to two of Bergen seven hills, Fløyen and Ulriken.

Ferries cross Vågen from Brygge

(below Rosenkrantztårnet) to the Nordnes peninsula, 7am–4.15pm on weekdays only. Other local boats serving the islands north of Bergen dock at Strandkaiterminalen, the inner harbour on the left-hand side of the fish market. The *Hurtigruten* (coastal steamer) and boats for fjords to the north leave from the Puddefjord inner harbour to the south-west of the centre. All quays are clearly marked in the *Bergen Guide* and on the local map.

Taxis: Bergen Taxi, tel: 07000. Bergen taxi and limousine service, tel: 55-21-99-25.

Cars: There is no particular advantage in having a car in the centre of Bergen, though the one-way system is well marked and effective. There is a toll charge, paid on entry to the city.

Outside Bergen, a car is more flexible than the bus, but is not a necessity. **Bergen Car Hire:** Hertz, Nygårdsgaten 89 (tel: 55-96-40-70); Avis, Lars Hillesgate 20B, tel: 55-32-01-30. **Breakdown Service**: Viking Salvage Corps, Inndalsveien 22, tel: 55-59-40-70. 24-hour service. NAF (Automobile Association), tel: 55-17-55-50.

Oslo/Bergen Cards

The **Oslo Card** gives free travel on virtually all public transport in the city, and suburban and NSB (main railway) trains within the Greater Oslo area. It also provides free parking in municipal car parks plus discounts on museum entrance prices. Price is 180–

410NKR. The **Oslo Package,** costing from 450NKR, offers accommodation and breakfast in over 44 hotels (all price ranges) and an Oslo Card. For time restrictions, check with the tourist office or visit www.oslopro.no.

The **Bergen Card** provides free admission to most museums, free transport and parking, discounts on sightseeing and shopping. Price 130–200NKR. The **Bergen Package** includes hotel accommodation (in over 20 hotel, with breakfast) and a Bergen Card. From 465NKR. All the above are available from Tourist Offices. Packages are available from travel agents.

ACCOMMODATION

Norwegian hotels are almost without exception of good standard. Geared to business use in the cities, they are expensive but provide swimming pools and fitness and other facilities. Almost all cut their prices dramatically from mid-June, through July and most of August, and also at weekends.

If you have been unable to reserve, the Tourist Information Centres in Oslo at Vestbaneplassen 1, tel: 22-83-00-50, for hotel booking tel: 22-33-06-40, and also the Tourist Information at Oslo Central Station, Jernbanetorget 2; tel: 22-17-03-95) will book accommodation for you, charging a small fee. In Bergen try the Tourist Information Office at Vågsallmenning 1 (tel: 55-32-14-80), opposite the fish market.

Oslo

Hotels vary in price from season to season and some offer special weekend rates, so be sure to double check the exact price when you book. Breakfast is almost always included in Norwegian hotels. A guide for two sharing per night: *$$$*: 1,500NKR and over; *$$*: 850–1,450NKR; *$*: less than 800NKR.

BRISTOL
Kristian IV's Gate 7
Tel: 22-82-60-00, fax: 22-82-60-01
Famous hotel, with ornate lobby and antiques in the bedrooms. *$$$*

HOTEL CONTINENTAL
Stortingsgaten 24/26
Tel: 22 82 40 00, fax: 22 42 96 89
Email: booking@hotel-continental.no
Website: www.hotel-continental.no
Each room in this elegant, luxury hostelry across from the National Theatre is individually decorated. The acclaimed Annen Etage restaurant provides *haute cuisine* dining, while the Theater Café attracts a loyal crowd of locals and visitors. *$$$*

FROGNER HOUSE
Skovveien 8
Tel: 22 56 00 56, fax: 22 56 05 00
Email: mail@frogner-house.com
A small, elegantly furnished place in the stylish West end. Service is helpful and the central location offers access to shops and restaurants. *$$*

GABELSHUS HOTEL
Gabelsgate 16
Tel: 23 27 6500, fax: 23 27 65 60
Email: booking.gabelshus@os.telia.no
This quaint, historic gabled hotel first opened its doors as a pension in 1912. It now offers modern comforts combined with historical furnishings and a fine in-house restaurant. *$$*

GRAND HOTEL
Karl Johans Gate 31
Tel: 22 42 93 90, fax: 22 42 12 2.
Situated on Oslo's main thoroughfa since 1874, this exclusive hotel has been the site for many Nobel prize celebrations and where visiting hea of state tend to stay. *$$$*

HOLMENKOLLEN PARK HOTEL
Rica Kongevn 26
Tel: 22-92-20-00, fax: 22-14-61-92
A traditional Norwegian building ne Holmenkollen Ski Jump, and only sor 15 minutes by underground train Stortinget. *$$$*

RICA HOTEL BYGDØY ALLÉ
Bygdøy Allé 53
Tel: 23 08 5800, fax: 23 08 58 08
Email: rica.hotel.bygdoey.alle@rica.r
This hotel in Oslo's stylish west en (10 minutes by bus from the city centre) re-opened after renovation and under new management in 200 Rooms are well furnished and servi is attentive. The popular Magma restaurant is next to the entrance. *$*

RICA HOLBERG HOTEL
Holbergsplass 1
Tel: 23-15-72-00, fax: 23-15-72-01
This hotel near the National Museum became part of the Rica chain in 2000. After extensive renovation, it now offers comfortabl well-equipped rooms. *$$*

RADISSON SAS SCANDINAVIA
Holbergsgate 30
Tel: 22-11-30-00, fax: 22-11-30-17
A 5-minute walk from the Royal Palac this hotel offers a swimming pool, ha salon, two restaurants and a bus servi to the airport (SAS check-in desk). *$$*

RAINBOW FROGNER HOTEL
Frederik Stangsgst 33
Tel: 23-27-51-50, fax: 23-27-51-40

This hotel in a quiet part of the Frogner quarter, just a 15-minute walk from downtown Oslo, has 64 well-equipped rooms with two floors reserved for non-smokers. *$/$$*

RAINBOW GYLDENLØVE HOTEL
Bogstadveien 20
Tel: 22-60-10-90, fax: 22-60-33-90
Comfortable B&B in the heart of the lively Majorstuen shopping district. *$$*

Bergen

Bergen hotels are only marginally less expensive than Oslo's but prices vary enormously throughout the year. The following categories cover two people sharing a double room, usually with a lavish breakfast. Price guides are as follows: *$$$*: 1,200NKR and over. *$$*: 600–1,200NKR. *$*: below 600NKR.

AUGUSTIN HOTEL
Sundtsgate 24
Tel: 55-30-40-00, gax: 55-30-40-10
This family-run hotel has comfortable rooms, some with views. Popular cellar bar. *$$*

CLARION ADMIRAL HOTEL
Sundtsgate 9–13
Tel: 55-23-64-00, fax: 55-23-64-64
This hotel, which has lovely, well-equipped rooms, looks over the harbour to Bryggen. Good restaurant. *$$$*

CROWDED HOUSE
Håkonsgaten 27
Tel: 55 23 13 10, fax: 55 23 13 30
Email: booking@crowded-house.com
Website: www.crowded-house.com
This renovated 'travel lodge' offers budget prices in a central location. All rooms are small, clean, simply decorated and have telephone and wash basin. (Toilets and showers in the corridor.) There is a laundry room and a kitchen with fridge. The Fusion kaffe bar downstairs is a hip, modern spot, serving great *espressos*, sandwiches and a decent breakfast. *$*

FIRST HOTEL MARIN
Rosenkrantzgaten 8
Tel: 53 05 1500, fax: 53 051501
Just minutes from the fishmarket, Bryggen and the Floybanen, this place has uniquely furnished, well-equipped rooms, a parking garage (fee payable) and two rooms with separate 'theme' rooms for children. *$$*

GRAND HOTEL TERMINUS
Zander Kaaesgate 6
Tel: 55 21 25 00, fax: 55 21 25 01
In a great location across from the train station, this elegant hotel has been a popular stopover for wealthy tourists since 1928. The comfortable room are beautifully decorated and the restaurant serves fine Norwegian cuisine with many dishes unique to Bergen. *$$/$$$*

NEPTUN HOTELL
Valkendorfsgate 8
Tel: 55 30 68 00, fax: 55 30 68 50
Email: office@neptun-hotell.no

A central hotel with 105 imaginatively decorated rooms. There are more than 700 works of art throughout the hotel, which creates a unique ambience. There are also two fine restaurants and the Ludvig Bar, known for its exotic cocktails. *$$/$$$*

HOTEL PARK PENSION
Harald Harfagresgaten 35
Tel: 55-54-44-00, fax: 55-54-11-44
This delightful, family-operated hotel with 40 specially decorated rooms is in the fashionable University quarter close to the city centre. *$$*

RADISSON SAS HOTEL NORGE
Ole Bulls Plass 4
Tel: 55-21-01-00, fax: 55-21-02-99
Email: guest@bgoza.rdsas.com
One of Bergen's most famous and well-loved hotels. Four restaurants including the gourmet Grillen. Night club, indoor pool, winter garden. *$$$*

RADISSON SAS ROYAL HOTEL
Bryggen
Tel: 55-54-30-00, fax: 55-32-48-08
Email: guest@bgozh.rdsas.com
Built into several old wharfhouses, with its entrance close to Bryggensmuseum. Good facilities. Airport bus. *$$$*

VICTORIA HOTEL
Kong Oscars Gate 29
Tel: 55 31 50 30, fax 55 32 81 78
This lovely 'bed and breakfast' hote is in Bergen's antique quarter an has impressive views of the hillto houses above. Rooms are simpl furnished, and the corridors of th historic building showcase ol photographs and paintings. *$$*

HEALTH & EMERGENCIES

No vaccinations are needed for you visit. Norway has reciprocal arrange ments for health treatment with mos European countries. From the UI obtain an E111 form from a Post Offic before you go. Charges are quite smal

Emergency Medical Treatment

OSLO: OSLO KOMMUNALE LEGEVAKT
Storgaten 40, tel: 22-11-80-80 (24 hour pharmacy)

BERGEN: EMERGENCY MEDICAL CENTR
Vestre Stromkai 19, tel: 55-32-11-2 (open 24 hours)

Emergency Dental Treatment

OSLO: OSLO KOMMUNALE TANNLEGEVAK
Tøyen Senter, Kolstadgata 18
Tel: 22-67-30-00
Weekdays 8am–11pm. Saturday, Sur day and holidays 11am–2pm, 8–11pm

BERGEN: VESTRE STRØMKAI
Tel: 55-32-11-20
Monday to Friday 4-9pm, Saturda to Sunday 3–9pm

Duty Chemist

OSLO: JERNBANETORGETS APOTEK
Jernbanetorget 4B, Oslo 1
Tel: 22-41-24-82 (24hrs)

BERGEN: APOTEKET NORDSTJERNEN
Bus Station
Tel: 55-21-83-84

Monday to Saturday 7.30am–midnight, Sunday 8.30am–midnight.

Emergency Telephone Numbers

Police 112

Fire 110

Accident/Ambulance 113

Police Lost Property (Oslo) 22-55- 55-64-60. Monday–Friday 9am–2pm.

Police Lost Property (Bergen) 113

ACTIVITIES

Skating

Oslo Kommune has around 150 winter skating rinks, where you can hire speed, ice and figure skates. Natural ice rinks are usually open from the beginning of December through March.

Curling

There are several curling clubs in Oslo that welcome members of foreign clubs. For details, contact Norges Curling Forbund-Rud, tel: 21-02-90-00.

Sledging

A horse-drawn sledge ride in the Oslo forest can be a highlight of any winter visit. Contact: Vangen Skistue, tel: 64-86-54-81. An alternative a guided ski tour or dog-sledge. For lunchtime and evening tours contact: Uten Grenser ANS, tel: 22-22-77-40, mobile: 90-87-16-21. In Oslo Forest, horse-drawn sleigh rides are available. Contact Polihestenes Venner', tel: 88-02-48-30, mobile: 94-22-38-52.

Trotting

A popular sport in both cities. Oslo's track is at Bjerke Travbane (tel: 22-95-60-00). Bergen's track is at Haukås in Åsane (tel: 55-24-79-00).

Swimming

Although you should not swim in Oslo's inner harbour, summer swimming in the fjord and off the islands is very popular. There are also many public pools including Tøyenbadet, an indoor pool at Helgensgt 90 and an outdoor pool at Frognerbadet, Middelthunsgt 28. Also, Bergen Pool, Sentralbladet Teatergt 37.

Amusement Parks

Oslo's newest attraction – Europe's steepest wooden rollercoaster, measuring an impressive 950m (3,117 ft) – is found at Tusenfryd Amusement Park, just south of the city. For further details, tel: 64-97-64-97.

Bergen Sports Clubs

Fishing

BERGEN SPORTSFISKERE

Fosswinekelsgt 37, tel: 55-32-11-64.

Tennis

BERGEN TENNIS PARADIS CENTRE

Paradis, tel: 55-91-26-00

Sailing

BERGEN YACHTING CLUB

Hjellestad Marina, tel: 55-99-14-00

USEFUL ADDRESSES

Norwegian Tourist Boards

UK

5 Charles House, Lower Regent Street, London SW1Y 4LR

Tel: 020 7839 6255

Fax: 020 7839 6014
Email: greatbritain@nortra.no
Website: www.norway.org.uk.

United States of America and Canada
655 Third Avenue, Suite 1810
New York, NY 10017
Tel: 212-885 9700, fax: 212-885 9710
Email: usa@nortra.no
Website: www.norway.org

Sightseeing and Tours

HMK SIGHTSEEING
Hegdehaugsvn 4, tel: 22-20-82-06
Sightseeing by coach around Oslo.

BÆTSERVICE SIGHTSEEING
Rådhusbryggen 3, tel: 22-20-07-15
Fjord sightseeing starting in Oslo.

HSD/FYKSESUND FJORDRUTER
Tel: 55-59-64-00
Day tours from Bergen.

BNR/BERGEN-NORDHORDLAND RUTELAG
Tel: 55-54-87-00
Tours north from Bergen.

GAIA TRAFIKK
Natlandsveien 89, tel: 55-32-77-00
Bergen bus tours.

FYLKESBAATENE I SOGN OG FJORDANE
Tel: 32-40-15.
Tours north from Bergen, including
'Norway in a Nutshell'.

HARDANGERTOUR
Tel: 55-59-64-00
Minicruise in Hardanger.

**HSD HARDANGER SUNNHORDLANDSKE
DAMPSKIPSSELSKAP**
C. Sundtsgate 36, tel: 55-23-87-00/80
Bus/ferry tours from Bergen..

WHITE LADY
Tel: 55-25-90-00/94-56-67-32
Bergen fjord sightseeing.

Tourist and Other Services

BERGEN KOMMUNE (local authority)
Bergen City Hall, tel: 55-56-62-00
Information office, 1st floor.

TOURIST INFORMATION CENTRES
● Vestbaneplassen 1, Oslo
Tel: 22-83-00-50,
Hotel booking: 22-33-06-40
● Jernbanetorget 1, Oslo Central
Tel: 22-17-03-95
● Bryggen, Bergen
Tel: 55-32-14-80

GUIDE SERVICE
● Oslo, tel: 22-41-48-63.
● Slottsgt 1, Bergen, tel: 55-32-77-0(
Also ask at travel agencies and Tour
ist Information Centres.
● Bergen Guide Service, Valkendorfsg
5, tel: 55-32-77-00.

NORWEGIAN TOURIST BOARD
Drammensveien 40, Oslo
Tel: 22-92-52-00

Embassies and Consulates

Oslo
UK
Ths. Heftyesgate 8, tel: 23-13-27-00
United States of America
Drammensv. 18, tel: 22-44-85-50

Bergen
UK
Carl Knowsgt 34, tel: 55-94-47-05

Useful websites
www.bergen-travel.com (Bergen site)
www.fjordnorway.no (the fjords)
www.flaamsbana.no (the Flåm railway
www.museumsnett.no (site on Norwe
gian museums)
www.norlandia.no (hotels on-line)
www.norway.org.uk (Norwegian gov
ernment site)
www.osloguide.no (all about Oslo)
www.tourist.no/www.visitnorway.co
(official Norwegian Tourist Board site

A

Amundsen, Roald 33, 34, 37
architecture 20, 21, 31–2, 48, 61
Askøy 55
Aurland 65

B

Baldishol Tapestry 12, 42
Bergen 8, 12, 30, 44–63, 72, 75, 77, 80,
   83, 84, 85, 86–7, 88–9, 90
   Aquarium 55, 57
   Bergenhus 50, 52
   Bryggen 48–50, 52, 85
   Bryggen Museum 48, 58
   Buekorps Museum 52, 57, 58
   Domkirken (cathedral) 52
   Fjellien 63
   Fjellveien 52, 63
   Fløyen 62–3, 85
   Frederiksberg Fortress 55, 57
   Galleriet 52, 53
   Gamle Bergen (Old Bergen) 54, 61–2
   Grieghallen 55, 56, 81
   Håkonshallen 50
   Hanseatic Museum 48, 49
   Historisk Museum 57
   Johanneskirken 56
   Korskirken 53
   Lille Lungegårdsvann 52, 56
   Mariakirken 49, 52
   Museum of Applied Arts 67
   National Theatre 55
   Naturhistorisk Museum 56–7
   Nordnes Peninsula 55, 57, 85, 86
   Nygårdshøyden 56
   Nykirken 58
   Puddefjorden 55, 85
   Rasmus Meyer's Collection 56
   Rosenkrantztårnet 50
   Schøtstuene 48, 49
   Sjøfartsmuseum (Maritime Museum) 5
   Stenersen's Collection 56
   Teatermuseum 57
   Tollboden (Customs House) 58
   Torgalmenningen 47, 50, 52, 53
   Torget 46, 47, 52, 53
   Vågen 47, 49, 55, 85, 86
   'White Lady' cruise 52, 54, 90
Bergen Express 51, 52, 53, 55, 84
Bergen International Festival 55, 56, 67,
   80–1
Bjørnson, Bjørnstjerne 14, 23, 55
Black Death 12, 17
Buekorps 57, 80
Bull, Ole 14, 55, 59, 66–7, 81
'Bybilleten' 46
Byfjorden 54
Bygdøy 31–5, 42, 74, 84

Fram Museum 14, 34
Kon-Tiki and Ra Museum 33, 34
Norwegian Folk Museum 31, 32
Sjøfartsmuseum (Maritime Museum)
15, 33
Sjømanskirke 33
Viking Ship Museum 10, 32–3

C

Christian IV 20, 27, 29
Christian Frederik, Prince 13
Christianity 10, 11, 17
churches 22, 33, 34, 49, 53, 56, 58, 59
concert halls 27, 30, 56, 59, 67
concerts 36, 39, 46, 56, 53, 59, 67, 81
Constitution Day 14, 16, 17, 80
cruises 24, 25, 52, 54, 89–90

D, E

Denmark 9, 12, 13, 14, 17, 20, 27, 50,
53, 54, 82
discos 26, 76, 77
driving 20, 77, 82, 85
Dronningen 31, 74
EC 16, 17
Eidsvoll 13, 17
Ekeberg 27, 81
Elsesro 54, 61
Eriksson, Leif 33

F

Fana Fjord 58
Fanakirke 58
Fantoft Stave Church 59, 60
Faroe Islands 54, 82
ferries 21, 54, 65, 66, 82, 84, 85
festivals 35, 55, 56, 67, 78, 80–1
Finland 83
Finnmark 10
Flåm 64, 65
folklore 30, 52, 58
food, Norwegian 35, 49, 51, 69, 70–2
Four Hundred Year Sleep' 13, 17

'Fram' 14,34
Frederik VI (of Denmark) 13
fur 69

G

Germans 12, 15–16, 17, 48, 49, 51
gold 11, 42, 43, 53–4, 69
Greenland 10, 11, 17, 33, 52, 69
Grieg, Edvard 14, 53, 56, 59, 81
Grimeland, Joseph 35
Gudvangen 65

H

Haakon VII 15, 16, 17, 29
Håkon IV 13
Håkon V Magnusson 9, 20, 29
Håkon den Gode 10
Håkon Håkonsson 12, 17, 50
Hanseatic League 12, 17, 48, 49, 75
Harald V 16
Harald Hårdråda 8, 17, 20
Harald Hårfagre 11–12, 17
Haraldshaugen 11–12
Hell 59
Heyerdahl, Thor 34
Hitler, Adolf 16, 29
Holberg, Ludvig 53
Holmenkollen 25, 36–7, 74, 81, 86
Festival 37, 80
Ski Jump 25, 36, 81, 86
Ski Museum 10, 37
hotels 22, 25–6, 35, 48, 50, 54, 65, 77,
85–7

I, J, K

Ibsen, Henrik 14, 15, 17, 23–4, 35, 59,
74, 86
Iceland 10, 11, 17, 82, 83
jazz 26, 30, 35, 74, 78, 81
Kalmar, Union of 13, 17
Karl Johan (of Sweden) 13, 17, 24
Kielland, Alexander 14
Kjosfossen waterfall 64

koldtbord 37, 60, 72, 73, 74, 75, 86
'Kon-Tiki' 33, 34
Krohg, Per 24, 35

L, M

Lapps 68
Lillehammer 81
lutefisk 72
Lutheranism 13, 17, 76
Lysefjorden 66
Lysøen 66–7, 81
Magnus Lagabøter 12, 17, 50, 53
Margrethe, Queen 13
Maridalen 81
markets 22, 43, 46, 47, 50, 52, 57
Michelsen, Christian 15
Munch, Edvard 23, 24, 39–40, 41, 56
Munch Museum 39–40

N

Nansen, Fridtjof 14, 33, 37
Nærøyfjorden 65
Nidaros cathedral 11
Nobel, Alfred 39
Nobel Peace Prize 23, 39, 81
Nordland 10, 37
Norheim, Sondre 37
North America 10, 14, 17, 33, 52
Norwegian Film Festival 81

O

oil 9, 16, 17, 52, 76
Olav V 16, 28
Olav Haraldson 10–11
Olav Kyrre 46, 48
Olav Tryggvason 10
Oskar II 14
Oslo 8, 12, 18–43, 72, 73–4, 76, 77, 80,
  83, 84, 85, 86, 88, 90
  Aker Brygge 9, 24–5, 42, 78
  Akershus Slot (Castle) 9, 16, 20, 25,
    27–8, 30
  Armed Forces Museum 27

Botanic Garden 39, 40
Bymuseum 38
Børsen (Stock Exchange) 27
Christiania 20, 27–8
Den Gamle Logen 27, 30
Det Gamle Raadhuset 28, 30
Domkirke (Cathedral) 22
Frogner (Vigeland) park 38, 86
Gamle Oslo 22
Historical Museum 42
Høymagasinet 28
Jernbanetorget 22, 84
Karl Johans Gate 21, 22, 80
Kunstnershus 81
Marka 36–7
Museum of Applied Arts 12, 42
Museum of Contemporary Art 29–30
National Gallery 41
National Theatre 23–4, 77
Nordmarka 36, 80
Pipervika 21, 32
Rådhuset (City Hall) 21, 41–2
Resistance Museum 16, 29
Royal Palace 20, 22, 24, 80
St Halvard's cathedral 22
Storting (parliament building) 13, 20,
  23, 86
Stortorvet 22
Studenterlunden park 22, 23
University 23, 30, 40
Vigeland Museum 38, 39
Oslofjord 20, 21, 32, 84, 88
Oslokartet 20, 85
Øvresetertjern lake 36

P, Q, R

Paradis 59
parks 22, 23, 30, 38, 56
population 10, 12, 17
Quisling, Vidkun 16, 17, 29
'Ra II' 34
Resistance 16, 29
Rjukan 16
Rosendal 81

S

Scotland 11, 50
Shetland Islands 54
shopping 42–3, 52, 53, 57, 68–9
sightseeing tours 60, 89–90
skiing 25, 36, 37, 63, 80, 81, 84
Sognefjord 60, 64, 89
South Pole 33, 34
Sørfjorden 64
Statsraad Lemkuhl' 48, 54
Stavanger 14, 16, 72
stave churches 32, 59, 60
Storting 13, 14, 16, 17, 22
Sturluson, Snorre 11–12
Sverdrup, Otto 34
Sweden 13, 14, 17, 29, 82
swimming 55, 57, 62, 63, 85, 86, 87, 88

T

theatres 23, 25, 46, 55, 77, 81

Tourist information offices 22, 46, 47, 51, 60, 84, 85, 89, 90
Tøyen 39
Tøyenhagen 39, 40
Troldhaugen 59, 60, 81
trolls 68
Trondheim 11, 80
Tryvannstårnet 36, 37

V, W

Vågen, battle of 53
Valdemar of Denmark 13
Vigeland, Gustav 38, 39, 40
Vikings 10, 11, 17, 32
Weideman, Jacob 30
Werenskiold, Dagfinn 22, 24
Wergeland, Oscar 13
wharfhouses 9, 24, 48, 50, 75, 87
wood carving 38, 69
World War I 15, 17, 35, 76
World War II 15–16, 28, 29, 35, 55, 65

ACKNOWLEDGMENTS

82	**B. & C. Alexander**
5, 14, 21, 22, 23, 24T, 28B, 39, 40, 42T, 52B, 79	**Hauke Dressler**
24B, 27, 30, 35, 42B, 43T, 61B, 65B, 68T, 72T, 83T	**Fritz Dressler**
46, 47, 48B, 53, 59B, 66, 67, 69B, 72B, 80, 84, 88T, 89	**Tor Eigeland**
Cover	**Greg Evans**
70	**Hans Klüche**
Back cover	**Blaine Harrington**
8–9, 10, 15T, 25, 31, 32, 33, 48T, 49, 54, 55B, 61T, 62–3, 76	**Nor-Ice Library**
20, 51B, 56B, 63, 83B	**Tony McCann**
4–5, 11, 16, 26, 34B, 37, 71	**Topham Picture Source**
56T, 64, 65T, 90	**Anthony R Dalton**
12	**Trygve Bølstad**
15	**Robert Meyer Collection**
77B	**Stefan Hanberg**
55T	**Terje Bergesen**
74T	**Nigel Tisdall**
Managing Editor	**Andrew Eames**
Design Concept	**V Barl**
Design	**Gareth Walters**
Cover Design	**Tanvir Virdee**
Cartography	**Berndtson & Berndtson**

NOTES